TOMORROW'S TRADE

PROBLEMS OF OUR FOREIGN COMMERCE

WHEN THE WAR ENDS

TOMORROW'S TRADE

PROBLEMS OF
OUR FOREIGN COMMERCE

Guide lines to America's future

as reported to

THE TWENTIETH CENTURY FUND

by

STUART CHASE

NEW YORK
THE TWENTIETH CENTURY FUND
1945

FOREWORD

THIS VOLUME is the fifth in a
series of reports written for the Twentieth Century Fund by Stuart
Chase to give the general reader a dynamic understanding of the
great issues of postwar America. Planned before Pearl Harbor,
the first four volumes in the series appeared while the war was on
and while most of the nation's energies were being poured into
the conflict. But even then the Fund believed that a clearer definition of goals for the peace would be a tonic for morale in war.

Now the war is over. We have been catapulted into the postwar world with unexpected suddenness. The problems Mr. Chase
set himself to explore in advance are no longer projections and
predictions but headline actualities. Mr. Chase's task has become
even more urgent than before.

The first volume of the series, *The Road We Are Traveling:
1914–1942,* was published in April 1942. In it Mr. Chase gave
his colorful interpretation of the sweeping changes in our social
and economic life which took place between the two world wars,
and laid down a sort of base line for a preview of the future.

In the second book, *Goals for America: A Budget of Our
Needs and Resources,* published in November 1942, Mr. Chase
put into ringing words the needs of the American people which

must be met to make a better world after the war and, using over-all figures of the goods and services these needs demand, he argued that we have ample man power and resources to produce them.

In *Where's the Money Coming From?*, published in November 1943, Mr. Chase carried the discussion one step further. He maintained that, not only shall we have the man power and plant to meet these postwar demands, but we shall be able to finance the full employment of our human and material resources.

However, in the fourth book of the series, published in January 1945 — *Democracy Under Pressure* — Mr. Chase pointed out that the United States must be united in fact as well as in name if this high destiny is to be fulfilled. He portrayed the drift toward monopoly in business, agriculture and labor, which is preventing us from achieving the maximum volume of employment and production and he indicted the great pressure groups for threatening to divide the nation by placing their own selfish economic interests above those of the public.

In the present volume Mr. Chase seeks to clarify the foreign trade and investment perplexities that must be dealt with, not tomorrow, but today. In the final book, *For This We Fought,* he will explore the larger issues which every shipload of returning veterans generates in the feelings and thoughts of millions of individuals. Apart from the personal problems of return to civilian life, the veterans are taking stock of the America they have come back to and the role they may collectively play in our national life. Mr. Chase will attempt to throw the light of his analysis on that process, the outcome of which means so much to all of us.

This series is designed to provoke thought and to stimulate discussion. Mr. Chase has been given entire freedom of authorship and he takes sole responsibility for all the material in this book.

However, in preparing the manuscript he has had the advantage of advice and criticism from members of the Fund staff and a number of outside consultants. But the opinions and conclusions expressed in these books are those of Mr. Chase. The Trustees and Fund staff take no position either for or against them.

Meanwhile, the Fund is carrying on one of its regular major research projects in the field of foreign economic relations — under the directorship of Norman Buchanan. The factual findings, and a program of policies to be formulated by an authoritative special committee on the basis of the research, are scheduled for publication in 1946. International cartels, which are, of course, interwoven with many other strands of our foreign economic relations, are being intensively studied in another current Fund survey. George W. Stocking and Myron W. Watkins are directing the research, and a special committee under the chairmanship of Dean James M. Landis of Harvard Law School will formulate the program for action.

In the field of financial and fiscal policy, which Mr. Chase explored in *Where's the Money Coming From?*, the Fund has recently published a volume giving the views of six leading professional experts. This volume, entitled *Financing American Prosperity: A Symposium of Economists,* contains contributions from the following authorities on the subject: B. M. Anderson, Professor of Economics at the University of California, Los Angeles; John Maurice Clark, Professor of Economics at Columbia; Howard S. Ellis, Professor of Economics at the University of California, Berkeley; Alvin H. Hansen, Littauer Professor of Political Economy at Harvard; Sumner H. Slichter, Lamont University Professor at Harvard; John H. Williams, Vice President of the Federal Reserve Bank of New York.

The Fund hopes that all these activities will contribute to a wide public understanding both of the unequaled opportunity in our peacetime reconstruction period and of the difficult problems it presents. The Fund is especially indebted to Mr. Chase for his challenging contributions to this end.

Evans Clark, *Executive Director*
The Twentieth Century Fund

330 West 42d Street
New York 18, N. Y.
September 1945

CONTENTS

1

LONG PERSPECTIVE

How ARE NATIONS going to ex-
change goods and services now that the war is over? War methods
are not "trade" at all, but rigorous government decrees designed
to keep goods out of the enemy's hands, and to smother him with
shot and shell. The methods of the twenty-year armistice from
1919 to 1939 were often restrictive, cumbersome and perverse,
with their sky-high tariffs, export subsidies and blocked currencies. Can we hope for better, fairer methods now that the
shooting has stopped?

I do not pretend to be a specialist in foreign commerce, but I
can follow a sack of flour as it travels by truck, boxcar and boat,
as well as the next man. Taking the reader firmly by the hand, we
will exert our joint powers of observation, and try to explore this
question together with a minimum of technicalities. Our guide
will be the economics of common sense. This is the standard
which guided us in the war, which guided us out of the depression, which the rest of the world will mostly use after the
war, and which we must learn to use. It goes below dollar signs,
and measures activity in terms of man power and materials.

The Man-Land Ratio

First, suppose we look at our planet from a long way off. Our small globe makes its way through illimitable space carrying some two billion human beings in its shallow curtain of atmosphere. Shallower still is the layer of humus soil on which all land life depends. If the processes of man-made erosion, now so magnificently under way, should reach their logical conclusion, life could be terminated as effectively as if a passing comet peeled off the atmosphere.

The planet's surface is about 196 million square miles. The United States covers three million, by way of bench mark. Almost three quarters of the whole surface is water, mostly salt, leaving only 55 million square miles of dry land, and 85 per cent of this lies north of the equator.

Not all the land is habitable. Knock off ten million square miles for polar ice caps and deserts. Knock off nearly half the remainder for the tundras of Siberia, and other inhospitable areas where life is one long fight. Brooks Emeny[1] estimates that no more than 35 million people, including the indefatigable Eskimos, live in the inhospitable regions. The overwhelming mass of mankind lives on the 25 million square miles or so of land where the humus is at least three inches thick. Even this is not all exactly inviting. A large fraction of it lies along the Amazon and the Congo, and in other fever-ridden spots where men, especially white men, die easily.

Most of the good lands, where men develop civilizations, lie in a band across the north temperate zone — Asia, Europe, North America. The corresponding southern bands are relatively small because of the tapering form of South America and Africa. Australia is a hollow shell with humus around a vast central desert.

1. *Mainsprings of World Politics,* Foreign Policy Association, New York, 1943. Most of the planetary figures here cited come from Mr. Emeny.

Eurasia holds three quarters of the world's population, concentrated in three chief centers of that single continental mass. China-Japan has 600 million, India-Burma 450 million, Europe without Russia almost 400 million. Hitherto these centers have been separated by deserts and high mountains, but now air transport is binding them together.

The population per square mile of arable land in Japan is 2,430, in Germany 587, in Italy 500. In the United States it is only 102, while in Russia it falls still further, to 68. There is land enough for all of us, more than enough as science advances; but obviously we have got to learn to live together on this limited soil with tolerance if not complete amiability. There is not enough to allow recurring waves of devastation in planetary wars, or savage onslaughts upon irreplaceable raw materials.

Integrated Communities

Nations today can be divided into three chief types:

1. Agricultural, such as China, India, Uruguay.
2. Industrial, such as Britain, Belgium, Germany.
3. Integrated, such as the United States, which can both feed itself and turn out the manufactured goods for high living levels.

Of the seventy-odd nations in 1939, most were agricultural, a few were industrial, none was integrated except the United States. Canada, with her industries stimulated by war, is now on the road to integration — but it is a nice point how far Canada has an economy separate from the North American complex. Russia is certainly on the way and in another generation may surpass the North American energy center. Her population, resources and arable land are all greater. Both China and India are candidates for integration; but no nation in Europe can aspire to it. A United States of Europe, however, might qualify. Its resources would be less than those of the United States, its population much greater, its arable land area (without European Russia) about the same.

The rewards of being an integrated community are self-evident. Any schoolboy could list them. Such a nation does not have to worry about its food supply the way the British, the Italians and the Japanese do. It is less nervous over the loss of strategic materials in the event of war. It can build up a balanced and flourishing internal market. It does not have to "export or die."

It is conceivable that future history books will rate only integrated nations as Great Powers. They alone have food, mass production and inanimate energy on a scale to fill the skies with battle planes, and so back up their foreign policies. On the other hand, it is conceivable that a world organization will, before too long, take over the battle planes and the atomic bombs and make the Great Power concept obsolete.

In 1835 de Tocqueville published *Democracy in America*. Andrew Jackson, the wild man from the border, was in the White House, and Nicholas I, governing a land of peasants and serfs — real legal serfs — was Czar of all the Russias. Looking a century ahead with extraordinary foresight de Tocqueville said:

There are at the present time two great nations in the world, which started from different points, but seem to tend toward the same end. I allude to the Russians and the Americans. . . . Their courses are not the same, yet each of them seems marked out by the will of Heaven to sway the destinies of half the globe.

The Russian army is a more powerful land force than the American in 1945, and the Russian foreign policy more definite and direct; but as a dynamic physical unit, the United States stands alone. Nothing like it has ever been seen. Take a long look, for nothing like it may ever be seen again. It is the result of a happy and accidental combination of forces, to wit: a prize location in the temperate zone, lavish natural resources, two protecting oceans, a wide-open frontier for many years, with plenty of opportunity for settlers, an immigrant population of individuals too restless and energetic to stay in the old country, a social structure without fixed classes.

Powerhouse

The United States has six per cent of the world's population living on seven per cent of the land area — two thirds of it pretty good land. The Mississippi basin has black soils as rich as those of the Ukraine.

As the war ends, America is producing around 60 per cent of the world's manufactured goods, both war goods and peace goods. She possesses 67 per cent of the fighting ships, 60 per cent of the battle planes, 70 per cent of the merchant ships, 75 per cent of the transport planes of the world. From her coal mines, oil wells and penstocks springs more than half the world's horsepower.

Before the war, even with eight to ten million unemployed, the United States held a commanding place in world economy. Here are some approximate ratios which I calculated in 1938:

Per Cent of World Total

Sulphur produced	78	Tons of RR freight moved	43
Motor vehicles produced	76	Steel produced	38
Rubber goods manufactured	67	Electric power	35
Petroleum produced	62	Coal produced	34
Corn grown	53	Copper ore produced	32
Cotton grown	50	Zinc smelted	30
Horsepower generated	50	Iron ore mined	29
Chemicals manufactured	43		

Since these figures were prepared the war has approximately doubled the American output. Some of the increases are fantastic. In 1939 we launched 460,000 tons of merchant ships, in 1943, 19,780,000 tons! Aluminum output rose from 327 million pounds to 2,257 million; magnesium from 7 million pounds to 392 million; synthetic rubber from 2,000 tons in 1939 to 900,-000 in 1943.

America has come out of the war unscathed by bombs. But all other major power centers — Germany, Japan, Russia, Britain, France, Italy — will be years digging out from the ruins of their cities, harbors, railroads, bridges, factories, transmission lines and dams. Thus the industrial lead which the United States possessed before the war will be greatly increased.

New Criteria

Our little swing into interstellar space made it reasonably clear that the United States is something different, something special, and something to be handled with gloves and a steel helmet. It hasn't very many people, relatively, on its three million square miles, but those people are full of mechanical know-how, all set around with fabulous prime movers. There is probably more mechanical power released in Pennsylvania in any given twenty-four hours than in all the mainland of Asia. We can knock the industrial spots out of Europe, which used to be the mainspring of industry. We can knock the industrial spots out of all the rest of the world combined. These incredible ratios of production may be impermanent, for we hold no copyright on either pure science or technology. Germany, for example, beat us to rocket propulsion. But they are the ratios which are operating as Japan surrenders. They are the ratios on which postwar world trade will first be built.

Our indicated role is to provide a kind of giant stabilizer. If we let the rest of the world alone it is likely to disintegrate further, involving us in endless conflicts. By the same token, if we drop into a serious postwar depression we shall drag the whole world down with us, so great is our economic leverage.

Classic theories of international commerce, developed when the United States was no greater industrially than Belgium, obviously will have to move over to make room for this leviathan. What was gospel and what was "sound" in the nineteenth century can hardly cope with 41 billion dollars' worth of Lend-Lease shipments, or with the economy which so blithely tossed them off.

Sometimes one wakes in a cold sweat, wondering what leviathan may do next. British men of affairs are said to be in a perpetual sweat. They fear America may not be able to coordinate its vast muscular economic body. Within a span of fifteen years its net national income has varied from $80 billion in 1929 to $40 billion in 1932, to $80 billion in 1937, to $160 billion in 1944 — which does not make much sense. Will it drop in half again after the war, with twenty million unemployed? Will our economy "turn out to be a giant with the mind of a child, devastating through mere inadvertence and immaturity?"[2] One hopes for the best. It is probably safer to be too strong than too weak.

However far leviathan may revise ideas and theories of foreign commerce in the years to come, one can still watch the movement of a sack of flour or a ton of bauxite. Stuff exchanged for stuff is the essence of our inquiry.

2. George Soule, quoting a British viewpoint, in *The New Republic,* March 5, 1945.

2

STUFF FOR STUFF

THE ELEMENTAL EQUATION

 Out of the mines, the farms, the factories of America comes pouring constantly a great river of goods. On V-J day, in 1945, it is nearly twice as great as it was in 1938, and a good half of it consists of tanks, guns and other war weapons. As we noted earlier, the part that comes from industry is about 60 per cent of the industrial output of the whole world.

In peacetime most of the stream finds its way into the homes and the plant of America. Only about six or seven per cent[1] of it flows outside the country, and of this a substantial part goes in trucks and freight cars over the border to Canada, a smaller amount over the Rio Grande to Mexico. The rest is loaded on a boat and dispatched overseas to the Caribbean, South America, Europe, Asia, Africa. After the war it is proposed that a lot be dispatched by sky trucks.

Before the war the export stream was running as follows:

1. In 1930, for instance, U. S. exported 7 per cent of her home production, imported 6 per cent of her consumption. But in Britain the figures were 25 per cent and 32 per cent respectively. Sumner Welles, *An Intelligent American's Guide to the Peace,* Dryden Press, New York, 1945.

	Per Cent
To Canada	16
Latin America	16
Europe	40
Asia and the Pacific	20
Africa and other	8

Total	100

The export stream, though only a fraction of our national product, is a sizable torrent in itself, with profound effects upon the rest of the world. The ten most important items in the years before the war, in order of value, were these:

1. Cotton
2. Tobacco
3. Petroleum
4. Fruits and nuts
5. Automobiles and parts
6. Copper
7. Meats and fats
8. Industrial machinery
9. Lumber products
10. Furs

All these products represent a great deal of hard work on the part of American farmers, sharecroppers, factory workers, managers, middlemen, transport workers.

Now let us turn and watch the parallel stream flowing into America. This also is a large torrent, as it should be. We are not looking at ledgers or bank balances; we are looking at physical goods and services. Does this incoming stream compensate for the stream going out? If it does not, over the years, then Americans are expending energy and exploiting resources without a fair return.[2]

The incoming stream just before the war was composed of the following ten major imports, in order:

2. The only measure we have for the two streams is an arbitrary one — money. Is an automobile *worth* more than a ton of copper? Who can say? We can only compare their prices in a single currency.

1. Coffee
2. Cane sugar
3. Crude rubber
4. Raw silk
5. Newsprint

6. Vegetable oils
7. Tin
8. Chemicals and drugs
9. Fruits and nuts
10. Furs

Note the whimsies of foreign trade, where we exchange furs for furs, and nuts for nuts. The incoming furs were mostly dressed, the outgoing undressed, if that helps any.

As one reads this list in 1945, the effects of the war are instantly apparent. Most of the items on it have grown scarce and some have been replaced. Crude rubber was import number three, and now we are using synthetic almost entirely. Raw silk was number four; rayon and nylon have mostly replaced it for the indefinite future. For tin, for drugs and chemicals, the war has created many substitutes. Soybean oil is no longer coming from Manchuria but from Illinois.

Twenty Years of Trade

Standing here and watching the two streams as they flow outward and inward, it is impossible to tell which is the greater. We shall have to go to the records for that decision — records that cover a period of years. Here, for instance, is a statement prepared by George N. Peek, formerly special adviser to the government on foreign trade. It summarizes all the transactions of Americans with other countries and other citizens from 1914 through 1933. It took many months to compile, yet it is so simple that any citizen bright enough to figure out his ration points can understand what foreign commerce means and how it works.[3]

3. The Department of Commerce has also published a balance sheet of payments since 1921.

From 1914 Through 1933

(*In Even Billions of Dollars*)

Americans sold goods abroad valued at about	90
They bought goods valued at	62
Leaving other countries in their debt	28
Other countries owed them for interest, freight, and other charges	11
Gross total owed to Americans in 20 years	39
Against which other countries paid Americans in gold	2
And charged Americans for entertainment of tourists, for remittances sent abroad by immigrants, etc.	13
Total offsets to bill	15
Leaving other countries in debt to Americans for 20 years' commerce	24

This debt was represented by:

War debts due from foreign governments to the government of the United States	10
Increase in loans and investments abroad by American citizens and corporations	14
Total as above	24

At the beginning of the period, in 1914, Americans owed to foreign countries a net balance of $3 billion. We were then what is called a "debtor nation," and had been since Plymouth Rock. Our canals, railroads, even cattle ranches, had been built in part by British, French and other European capital. We owed more abroad than was owed to us. By and large this meant that more goods had been shipped *in* to us than we had shipped out. After

1880 we began to ship out more than was shipped in, and the debit balance was whittled down.

Mr. Peek shows how we finally reversed the process, and became the greatest "creditor nation" on earth. The world owed us $24 billion on the twenty years' commerce. Deducting the $3 billion debit balance in 1914, the result works out to $21 billion net owed to us by the end of 1933. Ten billion was owed to the United States Treasury, and $11 billion net to private corporations and individuals.

The figures on the table look large — at least they would have looked large before we began spending $8 billion a month for war — but spread over twenty years, they are not so formidable. Exports averaged $4.5 billion a year, or around six per cent of our gross national income.

Invisible Items

Mr. Peek settles the problem of the size of the two streams with precision. We sent abroad $90 billion of goods and got back only $62 billion. If the dollar figures reflect tonnage — which, of course, they do not exactly — three shiploads would have gone out for every two coming in. But the table shows that this is not the whole story. If only visible goods counted, then the world would be $28 billion in our debt at the end of the period. We must also count in the so-called "invisible" items, before we strike a balance. The chief items are:

Freight charges. When Americans send goods to be carried in foreign ships, we pay for this service.

Marine insurance. Hitherto London firms have written most of this.

Tourists. When Americans travel abroad they must pay for food, shelter and entertainment. With the dollars so paid foreign nationals can buy American exports. Thus export of tourists has the same effect as imports of goods.

Remittances of immigrants. This has been a large item in the past. It will probably grow smaller and smaller, because for the past twenty years we have not admitted many immigrants. When Ivan Adamic sends one hundred dollars to his aunt in Yugoslavia, she exchanges them at the bank for local currency. Somebody else in Yugoslavia can then obtain one hundred dollars with which to buy American exports — cotton, automobile parts, tobacco, perhaps some of those mysterious nuts. Like tourist dollars, these immigrant remittances offset exports.

Interest and dividends to foreign holders of our securities. When Americans invest in, say, a Canadian company or a Turkish company, and when that company declares a dividend, Americans receive a credit on the international books, as in the case of an export shipment. Vice versa, when the Telephone Company pays its regular dividend, stockholders in London are credited with dollars, as if we had paid for British goods imported.

Diplomatic and consular expenses. These are akin to tourist traffic. The expenses of our government embassies and officials abroad release dollars and offset exports. The expenses of foreign officials in this country offset imports.

The Real Balance

During the twenty years from 1914 to 1933, outside countries owed us for invisible items $11 billion, while we owed them $13 billion. Thus the real size of the two streams emerges:

Total owed us for goods and services	$101 billion
Total which we owed	75 ”
Leaving the U. S. a creditor to the extent of	$ 26 billion

Our debtors knocked off $2 billion by sending us that amount of gold, leaving $24 billion as open debt. After 1933, we acquired a lot more gold, which we buried in Kentucky, as you know. Later we will discuss that gold.

The net result of this twenty years of foreign commerce was that America gave the world $26 billion more useful stuff than was returned to her. If gold be considered useful, then the net loss to the American community was $24 billion. The ratio runs about four to three. That is not a very healthy ratio. For a businessman it would mean sales of $75 against costs of $100. How long would he last?

Wait, you say; the $24 billion is a debt all right but is it not going to be some day repaid? Unfortunately it is not. The World War I debts have long since been defaulted, although not, I believe, officially repudiated. A large fraction of the private debt was defaulted during the depression. Some estimates run as high as $10 billion lost. Ask your friends about the future of their Polish, German and Peruvian bonds, if you are fortunate enough to hold no foreign paper yourself.

Most of the debt is a bad debt; and it is doubtful if we ever receive goods and services to cover it. In another frame of reference, however, the World War I debts might be considered as Lend-Lease advances to stop the Kaiser.

When the Peek table appeared, it was an open sesame of foreign commerce to me. Here in half a page of type were the major characteristics of all international transactions, in terms a person with a normal I.Q. could understand. Here were not only the flow of exports, imports, invisible services, gold shipments, war debts, but the net balance, so one could tell at a glance how his country, considered as a single organism, was making out in its dealings with the rest of the world.

Once a citizen grasps the meaning of this table and stations himself, as it were, on a high cliff above the shore line to watch the stuff roll in and the stuff roll out, the politicians, the professors, and the bankers can never tangle him up again. He thrusts the table in front of them and asks them to indicate specifically how their proposals will register there.

Imports First

Another approach through the jungle of technicalities is to make a simple analogy.

Here I live, the layman might say, in Middletown, U.S.A. If Middletown did not get considerable food and fuel from other parts of the country, people would soon be hungry and cold. Similarly, the country as a whole needs a lot of supplies from outside its borders — coffee, nickel, quinine.

Such a line of thought brings up the first major question: *What do we need to import as a community?*

Granting the community needs the item, we can hardly expect to get it on a Christmas tree, year in, year out. So the second major question arises automatically: *What can we ship in exchange for what we need?*

Here we have the theory of foreign commerce in its simplest aspect. Observe especially the order of the questions: *Imports first*. It has been customary to reverse the order and ask: Where can we dump our surpluses?

During the war, as we shall see, the exports-first formula was replaced by the logic of stark military need. Such traders as were not in uniform were shipping only to government license.

How about the postwar? The same logic is applicable in peacetime. The Bureau of Foreign and Domestic Commerce says: "Just as a high level of production is desirable chiefly as a means to a high level of consumption, so in the final analysis exports are important principally as a means of obtaining imports."[4]

Where Will They Get the Dollars?

After the war the big question will not be: Who wants our goods? but: Where will foreigners get the dollars to pay for our goods? Trade, as we have seen, is a two-way street. If a nation wants to sell, it must also buy — unless traders are to be replaced by Santa Claus.

Contrary to popular opinion, dollars which Americans spend for imports and for invisible items need not physically "leave the country." Dollar funds pass into foreign accounts of local banks, but these accounts are continually drawn on by foreigners for purchasing American goods and services. Thus these dollars re-enter the flow of the American national income.

Furthermore, the foreigner who receives the dollars does not himself have to spend them here. He can use them to buy foreign goods from another chap, willing to swap goods for dollars so that he, the third party, can get a new Buick or something else he desires from the U. S. This is so-called *triangular* or *multilateral* trading. Dollars may pass from country to country before they come back to pay for our exports.

Just before the war there was a good deal of *bilateral* trading, in which currencies and balances did not flow freely from country to country. Credits were "blocked." For instance, when Germans bought wheat from Yugoslavia, they gave the wheat grower a special kind of mark which was good only for a direct purchase in Germany. The British similarly issued blocked pounds when buying raw materials from Argentina.

4. Maffry and Lary, *Foreign Trade after the War*, October 1943.

Only as foreigners get dollars can our goods find markets abroad. There are just four ways a foreigner can get dollars:

> In payment for our imports.
> In payment for invisible services.
> As a loan.
> As a gift.

Look at the Peek table again; it is all there.

When the war loans went into default, many Americans agreed with President Coolidge when he acidly remarked: "They hired the money, didn't they?" People felt that Britain and France, as well-to-do countries, should honor their debts. It became a big political question. But if you have followed the argument thus far, you see why Britain, France and the rest could not pay in full. We would not take their paper money, and they had neither gold nor dollars for such a large payment. Their only possible ways to get dollars were either (1) to sell Americans more foreign goods and services, or (2) borrow dollars from American citizens to pay the American government.

We would not take the goods. Our tariff walls were already high, but in 1921, 1922 and 1930 we raised them higher. Foreign goods could not scale these walls in sufficient quantities to make a real dent in the war debts. Secondly, American investors finally declined to loan foreigners any more dollars with which foreigners would reimburse the U. S. Treasury.

President Coolidge was tripped up on the idea that "money is money," apparently not grasping the fact that francs and pounds are not dollars. He thought that if a Frenchman had francs he could pay his debts. But that, fortunately, is not the way foreign commerce works. I say fortunately, because if it did work that way, foreigners would need only to run their printing presses to buy up everything from Boston to San Francisco.

In a very real sense there is no such thing as "money" in international trade. We cannot be paid in dollars for what we export *unless we have first spent the same dollars for imports,* or loaned them abroad. Yet in the days of the great debate over the war debts of World War I, a Congressman insisted firmly: "We don't want their gold, we don't want their goods; we want their money." Twenty years later, a noted Congresswoman has come out against "reparations in kind" from Germany as proposed at Yalta, and demands "cold cash on the barrelhead."[5] When members of Congress go off the deep end in discussing foreign commerce, no wonder you and I have some difficulty in getting it straight.

"Favorable Balances"

Never let go of the idea that stuff must be exchanged for stuff. Without this touchstone foreign commerce passes into the realm of the occult. Without it, people otherwise certified as sane strive for a "favorable balance of trade," where the stuff of exports chronically exceeds the stuff of imports. A nation so endowed has a favorable collection of paper claims and an unfavorable leak in its stock of physical goods.

According to the *Encyclopaedia of the Social Sciences,*[6] communities of antiquity and city-states in the middle ages "were eager to retain within their borders as large a commodity supply as possible." Francis Bacon called this aptly: "The policy of plenty." The idea was to encourage imports as needed, but to restrain exports except as payment for needed imports.

The spread of money and credit gradually changed this and set up the reverse policy, in which it was thought more blessed to

5. Both cases reported in *The Nation,* March 10, 1945.
6. Article on "Protection" by E. F. Heckscher, Macmillan, New York, 1935.

give than to receive. Money was increasingly looked upon as the aim and end of trade. Imports became dangerous because they depleted the community of "treasure," i.e., domestic currency. Exports, on the other hand, were most worthy because they increased the "treasure." Thus the favorable balance idea grew up. Only with World War I, says the *Encyclopaedia,* "humanity returned to the view that goods are a blessing rather than a curse."

Another reason for seeking an excess of exports in recent years has been to provide more jobs at home. Our touchstone exposes this assumption as exceedingly dubious. As the excess of exports mounts, foreign buyers run short of dollars. The only way they can pay for our exports is to borrow dollars from us. This was done on a princely scale in the 1920's.

Observe the peculiar sequence:

American investors loaned dollars abroad.
Foreigners used the dollars to pay for American exports.
The exports stimulated production and employment in America.
But:
Foreigners got the goods, while
American investors lost their shirts.

When this sequence is straight in our minds, it suggests a blunt question: If employment must be subsidized, why not distribute the goods to people at home who need them?

Gifts Are Gifts and Trade Is Trade

As I will make plain later, I am not opposed to giving foreigners goods. Allies in war require mountains of guns. Both friend and foe after the war must have food, drugs and reconstruction supplies.

I am opposed, however, to calling such shipments "trade."

Trade is, or ought to be, a fair swap. Let us have things out in the sunlight. Let us call gifts gifts, and trade trade. At the same time we must not forget that sometimes gifts return to the giver many fold. We must not forget that the overpowering economic position of America as the war ends may necessitate some kind of free underwriting to preserve the world's stability — and our own. If employment must be subsidized, let us subsidize it honestly without a lot of hypocrisy about the necessities of export trade.

There is no particular virtue in what Jerome Frank calls "boatism" — just sending stuff abroad for the ride. Many citizens appear to believe that if we can only contrive to get our hard-won goods loaded on a boat, Utopia is here. . . . Which boils down to the axiom that the less we have the better off we are. Or, as Charles A. Beard once ironically put it to the author: "Some people think that Americans are bound to starve unless they can sell their wheat abroad."

Let me repeat the common sense formula:

> *The stuff we produce, as a nation,*
> *Plus the stuff we import,*
> *Less the stuff we export,*
> *Is a measure of our standard of living.*

3

JOURNEY THROUGH UTOPIA
THE CENTURY OF FREE TRADE

N OT ONLY FREE ENTERPRISE is celebrated in America today, but also its counterpart, world free trade. Some persons hold that this is primarily what we were fighting for, a free world without barriers to the flow of men, money and goods. Not a few believe that we lost a Utopia in World War I, and now are on the high road to regain it.

Mr. Cordell Hull has been the acknowledged leader of the free trade forces. He has not only spoken with eloquence, but in his reciprocal trade treaties he has acted. Tariffs on some commodities have been mutually lowered or abated. American bankers, after the Bretton Woods Conference in the summer of 1944, rebelled against the idea of planned world currencies. Many demanded a straight return to the international gold standard. American businessmen at the conference in Rye, New York, in the fall of 1944, warmly defended free trade and denounced cartels, against the raised eyebrows of foreign businessmen.

What was this Utopia which Americans hold in such veneration? First we will examine the theory of free trade (including, in the next chapter, its corollary, the gold standard). Then we will take a look at the economic practices of the nineteenth century. Finally we will try to appraise the prospects of reviving these methods in the world of 1950.

Each Cobbler to His Last

Broadly speaking, the theory of free trade contemplates the whole world — or at least its habitable parts — as a single productive unit. Here is coal, there is iron, yonder is copper. Here wheat grows best, here cotton, over there coffee. In this community people are skillful at weaving textiles; in that at smelting steel. Let each nation produce what it has available at low cost, whether because of climate, national resources or popular skills, exchanging the output with the low-cost products of other nations. In this way everyone exerts his talents in the direction where they have the greatest scope, and all the world falls heir to the fruits of these especially nourished abilities. There must of course be no artificial barriers to this salubrious exchange.

Interdependence and specialization were recognized even by the Mercantilists. Said one of them, Gerard Malynes, in 1601: "God caused nature to distribute her benefits or His blessings to severall climates supplying the barennesse of some things in our country with the fruitfulness of other countries, to the ende that enterchangeably one commonweale should live with another. . . ." A charming exposition of the theory of free trade, which has not been improved on to this day.

Universal free trade was justified on the ground that the maximum economic interest of each nation was identified with the maximum economic interest of the whole world. Adam Smith, who was a practical reformer rather than a pure theorist, did indeed admit that governments might have to protect certain industries in the interest of na-

tional defense. But such derogations seemed to him and to his follow-
ers trivial exceptions to the rule.[1]

Thus the harmony of interests propounded by the classical
economists for individuals on the home market was extended by
analogy to nations on the world market.

The Real World

In liberal theory, Great Britain was merely another nation
dealing on the world market, but the outstanding fact in the real
world of the nineteenth century was the *towering place* of Britain.
She was the leviathan then; she maintained a policy of free trade
singlehandedly against the world, and had the power to enforce
it. When the power declined, the policy withered.

The United States on the other hand has never been a free trade
country, right back to the days of George Washington. The Constitution forced Connecticut to take down its tariff barriers against
New York, and gave us internal free trade between the states.
Externally we have always had tariff duties on many commodities,
mostly stiff ones. The Republicans are supposed to make them
stiffer, the Democrats slightly less stiff. Nobody with political
power has seriously proposed to abolish them altogether. Free
traders, like socialists and single-taxers, make a lot of noise; but
in 157 years they have never got to first base. This does not mean
that we cannot some day burn down our customhouses. It simply
means that if there is such a thing as an American tradition, this
is it.

On December 5, 1791, Alexander Hamilton sent his famous
Report on Manufactures to the House of Representatives. It was

1. E. H. Carr, *The Twenty Year Crisis, 1919–1939,* Macmillan, London,
1939.

one of the ablest arguments for protecting "infant industries" ever prepared. Advocates of protection in the United States and Europe during the nineteenth century "were united in their eagerness to ward off British competition by erecting tariff walls. They looked upon British free trade as a means of reducing all other nations to hewers of wood and drawers of water, and upon British sponsorship of international free trade as a Machiavellian trick by which England had reached her supremacy. The only way to attain equal status with Britain was thought to be protection. . . ."[2]

Yankee Traders

International trade was as important to America, up to 1850, as it is to Belgium today. We exported chiefly raw materials — cotton, tobacco, lumber, wheat — and imported many manufactured goods. Our imports by value always exceeded our exports, and we paid for them by earnings of our clipper ships, by our newly-mined gold, by borrowing abroad.

After 1850, the pattern began to change. We exported more and more manufactured goods, and began to import raw materials for our new industries. Soon a vast inland market began to form, stretching from the Atlantic to the Pacific. The relative importance of foreign commerce declined.

It is interesting to recall details of how we traded in the good old days when our balance was always "unfavorable." Here is a typical case:[3]

The *Morea* was a full-rigged ship of 330 tons built at Charleston, Massachusetts, in 1828, and owned by the firm of A. and C.

---

2. *Encyclopaedia of the Social Sciences,* article on "Protection," by E. F. Heckscher.

3. Described by Captain John Codman in *The American Neptune,* October 1942.

Cunningham of Boston. In 1839 she was fitted out for the East India trade. According to custom, the owners put part of the outward-bound cargo on board for their own risk and venture, but the balance consisted of "adventures" by the captain, the supercargo, the mates, members of the crew, and various outsiders. These "adventures" gave the crew a keen interest in the voyage and greatly helped morale and discipline.

The chief items loaded in Boston were cotton cloth, potatoes packed in sand, raisins, dried New England apples, cider, Medford rum, glassware, flour, pilot bread, tobacco, cheap jewelry, bacon, furniture, clocks, crockery and Yankee "notions" of all kinds. All the cargo was consigned to the supercargo — something like the purser of today — for "sales and returns." He normally sold the goods of each party abroad, received foreign currency, and invested the proceeds in the return cargo, pro rata for each adventurer — a chest of tea, a bag of coffee, a picul of tin. These goods were turned over to the adventurer at the end of the voyage. He either took them home or sold them on the Boston market.

The *Morea* disposed of her 1839 cargo at Singapore, took a load of betel nuts to Macao, which proved enormously profitable. Then she filled up with chests of tea and bolts of silk at Hong Kong, dodging a naval battle in the Opium War between Britain and China as she cleared the harbor. Messrs. Cunningham netted $100,000 on the voyage! The adventurers also made handsome profits, in spite of whatever duty they paid. Though not strictly free trade, the whole set of transactions was private enterprise in the classic sense.

Mistress of the Seas

Britain had a long head start in the industrial revolution. She was indeed the workshop of the world for many decades, and "Britannia rules the waves" was no Chamber of Commerce boast. She had two centuries of tough seafaring experience behind her when James Watt perfected his steam engine in 1776. She had an energetic, commercially-minded population, rapidly increasing, and a landed gentry too weak to preserve the feudal status quo. She had a politically mature governing class. She was the natural leader in the first dizzy upswing of the machine age.

Power is essential to every political order. There must be a sheriff or there is no order. The British fleet not only guaranteed immunity from major wars, but policed the high seas and offered equal security to all honest traders. The London money market established a single-currency standard for virtually the whole world — sterling backed by gold. British merchants secured — for a time — a wide acceptance of the principle of free trade, and they established world market prices for wheat, cotton, sugar and other staples. English became the commercial language of four continents.

"These conditions, which were at once the product and the guarantee of British supremacy, created the illusion — and to some extent the reality — of a world society possessing interests and sympathies in common."[4] Thus a kind of world state was actually operating, with Britain supplying the rules, the money mechanism and the police power. Free trade was a function of that one-power sovereignty.

The Era of Free Trade

From the repeal of the navigation laws in 1849 to the Bismarck tariff acts of 1880, free trade was expanding over the world. This

4. E. H. Carr, *op. cit.*

was its period of triumph. The first victories were on the home front. In 1839 Richard Cobden and John Bright had organized the Anti-Corn Law League in Manchester, and begun a campaign so spirited and eloquent that we still read with relish their dissertations. The Corn Laws levied a tariff on grain. It was Sir Robert Peel who succeeded in getting it withdrawn in Parliament in 1846, and in taking restrictions off navigation in 1849. This left Britain with her foreign trade substantially free of customs duties and other barriers.

Free trade was warmly supported by British ironmasters and textile manufacturers, who were so far ahead of the rest of the world that they did not fear competition on finished goods, but wanted their raw materials duty free. The policy fitted them like a glove. To change Britain from a semi-agricultural to an all-out industrial nation seemed highly desirable to everyone — except possibly the surviving farmers.

Other European countries climbed aboard the bandwagon. Holland reduced her tariffs in 1845, Belgium repealed her corn laws in 1850. By that year Britain was the principal supplier to the world of nearly all staple factory-made products — textiles, ironware, crockery and the like. In return she imported food for her mill workers, and raw materials for their machines.

Her navy was on a two-power standard, ready to fight on equal terms the next two strongest fleets. In the 1870's, British exports exceeded those of the next two largest exporting nations combined. This was the apex.

A general system of free trade was never achieved. As Carr points out, Britain was the only country in Europe powerful enough to act according to the international harmony of interests, where each nation produced what it could most cheaply. The United States never practiced it, as we have noted. Frederick List, the great economist, told the Germans in mid-century that free trade was fine after one got to be a big boy, but not so good while one was growing up. Bismarck carried out List's prescription with the tariff acts of 1880. France put up a high wall in 1892. Hardly were the British dominions given their independence when they proceeded to protect themselves against the manufacturers of the mother country.

Waning Power

This curious unilateral structure could hardly have lasted. The machines bred too rapidly. Britons were not the only people who could swing a spanner or follow a blueprint. Their adventure in expanding free trade about the world was short-lived, and their monopoly of power almost as short.

By the turn of the century competition in foreign trade was promoting a fierce imperialism. In 1903 Joseph Chamberlain led a powerful opposition in Parliament, and came close to putting over a protective tariff in Britain itself. By 1913, both Germany and the United States were exporting as much as Britain, while the industrial production of Germany was as great, and that of the United States twice as great. When the German army invaded Belgium in 1914, free trade went into a permanent eclipse.

The Boer War in 1900 first demonstrated to the world the decline of Britain's military might. A few Dutch homesteaders with rifles repeatedly defeated regiments of the line. By 1914, British pre-eminence remained in shipping and finance alone. World War I was to undermine both. The monopoly of power was shattered.

The Incredible Century

Nobody has yet given an adequate account of the causes which produced the rapid expansion of the nineteenth century. Why did the population of the world double, and that of the West increase fourfold? What furious dynamo was at work? There had never been such a growth rate before, and probably never will be again.

Were free trade and free enterprise responsible? In part they probably were, although most nations did not enjoy free trade and free enterprise.

Were tariffs responsible? In part, by helping the establishment of factories in other places than England.

Was the British navy responsible? In part, because it cleared the seas of pirates, and maintained safe passage for the exchange of goods.

Was the gold standard responsible? In very small part, as we shall describe in the next chapter. It helped London to operate a world currency for a time, which in turn helped trade.

Was technology responsible? Now we are getting somewhere! In my opinion, the application of science had more to do with nineteenth century expansion than all other causes combined. The dynamics of the century was connected with inanimate energy, running over into the veins of men.

While we cannot be sure how far the British free trade era helped expansion, we can be certain that expansion helped free trade, and in three specific ways:

1. When markets expand as rapidly as they did up to 1880 or so, there is room for most producers. Demand is chronically ahead of supply, and competition is not too fierce. Such a condition is wonderful for trade.

2. As new frontiers were broken out for settlers in five continents, poor people were given such opportunities as had never before been known. Also freedom of migration made a fine background for freedom of trade.

3. The growth of population encouraged constantly rising land values, which created a sense of confidence in the present and the future. One bought in on the 1850 level and sold out on the 1880 level, almost always at a profit. Like operators on the New York stock market from 1926 to 1929, one had to be something of a genius to lose.

The Royal Institute of International Affairs summed it up: "It was the continual widening of the field of demand which, for half a century, made capitalism operate as if it were a liberal utopia." Karl Mannheim adds a homely illustration: Traffic control is unnecessary, he says, so long as the number of cars does not exceed the comfortable capacity of the road. Until the fenders begin to crumple, it is easy to believe in a natural harmony of interest between motorists.

The Expansion Rate

The following figures give an indication of the growth rate of the incredible century.[5]

Year	Total World Trade (In Billions of Dollars)	Per Cent Share			
		United Kingdom	United States	Germany	France
1840	2.8	32	8	–	10
1860	7.2	25	9	–	11
1880	14.8	23	10	9	11
1900	20.1	21	11	12	8
1913	40.4	17	15	12	7
1929	66.7	14	14	10	6

5. Tables from the *Encyclopaedia of the Social Sciences,* article on "International Trade," by Franz Eulenburg.

Observe the colossal rate of growth in total trade, the steady decline of Britain's share after 1840, of France's after 1880, and the rise of the United States and Germany. Meanwhile the dependence on foreign trade of Britain and other industrial nations is shown in these figures:

Foreign Trade Per Capita in Dollars, 1929

Denmark	266	Germany	100
Holland	243	United States	79
Switzerland	228	Japan	32
Britain	219	Russia	6
France	103		

Summary

Free trade is defined as the type of trade that prevails inside the United States. With world free trade, a Ford car would cost the same in Shanghai as in Michigan, plus the undoctored freight charge. This would be a desirable state of affairs in many respects. How do we get it in the United States? Looking about us we find three institutions which are not discernible in the world at large: *a cop, a court and a currency.* There is no international money system, no real international law, because no international police power exists to enforce it. Governments sign treaties and agreements which some of them, a few years later, take a perverse delight in tearing up. Anarchy tempered by promises has been the rule in international affairs for longer than one cares to remember.

For a few decades in the nineteenth century, the British Empire was powerful enough to provide for the world in some degree the condition found inside the United States. Her navy became a kind of world sheriff, her merchants set up trading rules which were widely observed. The City operated a gold standard which served for a time as a world monetary unit. Cop, court and currency were present.

The police power faded out with the Boer War. The trading rules could not stand against the onrushing competition of the United States and Germany, with their tariff-protected industries. The pure gold standard went out while the central banks were coming in, as we shall presently see. Only with the utmost difficulty did Britain maintain a policy of free trade up to 1914.

All of which raises an interesting question in both logic and scholarship: How far is it permissible to generalize about the eternal verities and the practical benefits of world free trade, in the light of such a very special case?

4

GOLD—THE JOURNEY CONTINUED

THIS CHAPTER is mostly about the international gold standard, its rise and fall. It fell much earlier than most people think. You can skip the chapter if you like, for the subject is chiefly of historical and, shall we say, theological interest. I doubt if the pure standard will ever be used again. Its purpose was to achieve stability. In the end it failed in that purpose.

The gold standard, in the sense of a kind of world currency, was part of the theory of free trade. Free trade was also dependent on some armed force to keep the peace. According to J. P. Wernette, the gold standard was due to various historical accidents, and its wide adoption in the nineteenth century was due to England's lead.[1] As we have seen, she was the leader in practically everything until the United States and Germany began to catch up with her.

Fundamentally the gold standard is not hard to understand, although the subject can run into great theoretical complications. Each nation, as you know, has its own money system, a currency

1. *Money, Business and Prices,* King, London, 1933. Mr. Wernette, now teaching at Harvard, will be our chief guide through this section.

with a standard unit — a dollar, a pound sterling, a ruble. Every time you cross the border into Canada or Mexico you are instantly made aware of this fact. In the past, the currency usually consisted of a dependable amount of some useful commodity, such as rice, furs, copper, gold. Gold became the favored commodity for various reasons. It is convenient to handle and measure, and almost impervious to physical depreciation. When Britain adopted it as the official standard, the pound sterling was equated with 113 grains of gold. In the United States somewhat later the dollar was equated with 23 grains of gold. You could take your paper currency to the bank and get that weight of gold.

The International Standard

If two nations are on the domestic gold standard as above, and allow free exchange of gold and foreign currencies, they will have a *parity of exchange,* arrived at by dividing the gold weights to which the monetary unit of each is equated. Thus when the pound sterling is equated at 113.001, and the dollar at 23.22 grains of gold:

Parity is $\dfrac{113.001}{23.22} = 4.86$, or a pound sterling will buy as much gold as four dollars and 86 cents will buy. You could go to a London bank, slap down a £100 note and get a bag of gold just the weight of the bag you would get from a New York bank if you counted out $486 in paper money.

This hitches the pound to the dollar in an intimate way, and we have the beginning of an international currency. If all nations join the standard by voluntary agreement, we go a long way toward an international currency. Everybody's money exchanges with everybody else's at dependable ratios; variations from parity will seldom be great. This does not mean that a gentleman in

Poland could always get dollars if he had plenty of zlotis. It merely means that when he had to settle a bill he knew what basic ratio between zlotis and dollars he could figure on.

The parity of exchange achieved by gold helps international buyers, sellers, lenders, borrowers, to know what to expect when their contracts come due. If a country is not on the standard, the rate of exchange between currencies depends on supply and demand, and can fluctuate widely. The rate is arrived at like odds on a pari-mutuel horse race, at such a level as to clear all the money at that level.

The claims of one nation are balanced off against another, debit and credit, something like bank checks in the clearing house in a large city. Any balances remaining after such international clearing are supposed to be settled by a shipment of gold. Thus if a country's imports are running consistently ahead of her exports, she must ship gold to settle the balance. If she hasn't enough gold, and can get no credit, she will be driven off the gold standard. No longer will the central bank buy gold from anyone and sell to anyone, in any amount, at a fixed price; or allow gold to move into the country or out of it without restriction.

The stability of foreign exchange rates, in the opinion of Mr. Wernette, is the principal advantage of the international standard. And it is a very considerable one, especially for investors in foreign bonds and other long-term contracts.

The Terrible Choice

Unfortunately there are also serious disadvantages. The international gold standard tends to affect the whole economic life of the subscribing country, particularly if it does a relatively large foreign business. A nation surrenders part of its independence when it agrees to abide by an automatic mechanism outside its control. Britain, Belgium, Switzerland, Denmark, Holland are particularly vulnerable; the United States not so much, Russia still less.

If for any reason a country is losing gold steadily, its monetary authorities are in duty bound to take the severest action to halt the outward flow, like a doctor whose patient is in danger of bleeding to death. The order of treatment has been to:

> Reduce imports
> Stimulate exports
> Reduce costs
> Reduce prices
> Reduce wages
> Reduce incomes
> Reduce spending

These measures all tend to keep money from leaving the country, or to encourage foreign currency to come in; but they are heroic medicine. They sound a clear invitation to depression in the home country. The gold standard is saved at the cost of unemployment.

The dilemma has been responsible for some famous historical decisions — whether to cling to gold and respectability, at the cost of internal hell and damnation, or to lose face and avoid depression. Britain went off gold in September 1931, dragging the whole sterling bloc with her, because the government did not dare impose further hardships on its people.

France, after putting her people through the wringer repeatedly and heroically, went off gold in 1936, taking the rest of the gold standard nations with her.

I think it fair to ask: how useful is a mechanism which presents a people with such a dreadful choice?

Gold Fields

For economists like Professor Kemmerer of Princeton, the real Golden Age was from 1821 to 1914, while Britain maintained the full gold standard. Certainly this was a time of great expansion, as we have seen. It was also a time of gold strikes — California, Australia, Alaska, South Africa. Without these lucky strikes and the contribution they made to the metallic base of the world's currencies, expansion might have been halted, or else the gold standard would have been widely abandoned, as it was after 1914. The United States almost left gold at the turn of the century, as the Peerless One thundered for free silver. "Probably," says Keith Hutchison, "it was only the discovery of the Rand that saved the day and kept Bryan out of the White House."[2]

Fetish

Sometime after the turn of the century, the gold standard, both international and national, lost its practical utility and became a kind of fetish — like the high silk hat of the London businessman a generation ago. If you did not have it, you were not presentable. It ceased to be defended on rational grounds, as a mechanism for achieving price stability. The original end of stability was forgotten in pious obeisance before the golden means.

Wernette observed in 1932: "That the adoption of any particular relief program might drive the United States off the gold standard is considered complete and final proof that the program is very, very bad." Gold was a sacred symbol, like the home, motherhood, and success, "only to be questioned by fanatics, traitors and fools."

This violent emotional attachment is the more curious in that the international gold standard had long ceased to exist as an auto-

2. *The Nation*, February 2, 1945.

matic stabilizer. With the rise of the Central Banks, regulating the national banking system and cooperating with the Treasury, monetary authorities began to "manage" gold, and thus inject human volition into a mechanism supposed to be as automatic as a thermostat.

It was precisely this thermostat quality which gave well-to-do people confidence. Here was something, they thought, which politicians could not monkey with. Time after time in past centuries creditors had been wiped out in ruinous inflations by printing-press money. The gold standard was thought to make such inflation impossible. Debts would be honored at par so long as it held fast.

But many years before World War I, the gentlemen in charge of the Central Banks began tinkering with the thermostat. The adulation continued undiminished. Even after the dreadful experiences of the interbellum period, veneration continued, and it continues right up to the present day. A large section of the financial community at this moment in America demands a return to gold. Elsewhere the attitude is less pious. Said the London *Economist* in 1941: "The pull of a metallic standard and of immutable mint parities has probably ceased to operate forever."

"Managing" the Standard

The international gold standard, rigidly adhered to, demanded deflation of the domestic economy, as we have seen, whenever gold began to leave the country. Central banks, says Polanyi, fortunately mitigated this threat. They *managed* the standard, but slowly, fearfully, often with a sense of moral guilt.[3] "Manipulation was substituted for the self-regulating mechanism of sup-

3. *The Great Transformation,* Farrar and Rinehart, New York, 1944.

plying credit, even though the device was not always deliberate and conscious."

Professor Jacob Viner, writing in the *Encyclopaedia of the Social Sciences,* comes to the same conclusion. While the international gold standard is automatic in theory, he says, no such thing exists in practice. In the practical world the standard has been managed.

Wernette emphasizes the point. No careful student of the problem believes that local currency and gold were kept in a stable relation by purely automatic processes; "manipulation is part of the system." He proceeds to follow this idea to its logical, and shocking, conclusion. If manipulation is necessary in the case of the gold standard, as well as in the case of the paper standard, why fool around with gold at all? Why not manipulate directly? That, of course, is precisely what the "managed currency" school advocated, and what every government on earth now does in 1945.

It has taken a long time to get it out in the open and be honest about it. "After 1914," says Knud Fick, "one nation after another found herself obliged to abandon the gold standard — some for a time, and some forever; a few in plain terms, but most of them in fantastically involved circumlocutions."[4] Britain fought her way back to gold in 1925, hung on for a few painful years, and fell off with a great moral explosion in 1931. Polanyi believes that this is the date historians will use to mark the end of the nineteenth century international system.

Carr's testimony on the matter of managing the standard is definitive:[5]

Modern talk of "managed" trade and "managed" currencies sometimes carries with it the implication that nineteenth century trade and

4. *Journal of Accountancy,* December 1943.
5. *Conditions of Peace,* Macmillan, New York, 1942.

currency required no management. . . . This is an illusion. The international trade of the nineteenth century was "managed" by the merchants of Great Britain. . . . The international currency was "managed" by the city of London, which discounted bills, made loans and advances, adjusted exchange values and arranged the necessary minimum transfers of gold. London ceased to play this role in 1914 and has never regained it, and cannot now regain it. Failure to find some other orderly method of conducting and financing international trade, or even to perceive that some other method was required, has been responsible for the economic and financial anarchy of the ensuing period. After twenty-five years it is time to understand that international trade and finance must be organized on a new basis, and that nineteenth century precedents are valueless and misleading. Counsel has too long been darkened by idle dreams of a return to free trade, or a restoration of the gold standard.

In 1944, John Maynard Keynes told the House of Lords that after twenty years he had succeeded in establishing three principles essential to the economic stability of his country. They were:

1. That the external value of the pound sterling shall conform to its internal value as set by Britain's own domestic policies, rather than the other way round.

2. That she will retain the control of her domestic rate of interest, to keep it as low as suits her purpose.

3. That she will not accept deflation and unemployment at the dictate of influences from outside.

Lord Keynes is not only the greatest living economist, but as head of the Bank of England he has been the most powerful financial figure in Britain. In the face of this statement, a return to the international gold standard seems remote.

History Does Not Run Backward

The trouble with the gold standard, as well as with free trade, was that both were mechanisms which worked well *only under special circumstances.* They were capable of universal generalization in theory but not in practice. In practice both broke down when exposed to wilder winds than the snug protection of Britain in the middle of the nineteenth century. Without tariffs, some other nations would not have developed their industries. Without managed currencies, the condition of some local economic systems would have become intolerable.

Free trade and the gold standard have often been treated in the literature as absolutes. It is now clear that they are nothing of the kind. They are mechanisms, means to an end. The final end is presumably the welfare of mankind. The approximate ends are employment, rising living standards, and enough stability and contentment in the several nations to keep them from assaulting their neighbors. Depending upon conditions, various mechanisms have been appropriate for these ends — free trade, protective tariffs, the gold standard, managed currencies. Appropriateness varies with time and place.

"Under modern conditions," says John H. Williams, "the gold standard has frequently not been the efficient instrument of two sided complementary international adjustment it was meant to be. It has been a means of spreading depression and sometimes booms, from one country to another. One of the great defects of gold standard theory has been its failure to take account of the business cycle . . . it took full employment for granted."[6] This is the great defect in classical economic theory in general; it thought a special case was a general case. Einstein made no such mistake with his two theories of relativity.

Mr. Williams takes a look at the U. S. leviathan, as we tried to do in the first chapter, and observes that the United States is one

6. In *Papers and Proceedings* of the American Economic Association, January 1944.

of the main reasons why the gold standard cannot work as originally intended. We are so big, so self-contained, that we do not need to play the golden game. We like to export, but we hate to import, and so we limit our imports. Three quarters of all the gold in the world came to us during the thirties in lieu of imports. According to theory this should have created a roaring boom in the United States. It did not do so, but it spread deflation and despair throughout the gold shipping nations.

Seven Hurdles

Free trade is in a different category. We know now, or ought to know, the conditions in which to expect it, namely, a world state with a world police force, or a substitute like the British navy in 1870. We ought to know that without such an international political structure, national agreements to abolish tariffs are likely to meet the fate of the Kellogg pact to abolish wars. As there has been no power in the international field charged with creating order and economic harmony, "the temptation," says Carr, "to assume a natural harmony is therefore particularly strong."[7] Such harmony is a snare and a delusion, a mental trap into which wishful thinkers can fall headlong.

Failing a world cop, court and currency, there are at least seven substantial reasons why a given country at a given time might renounce free trade:

1. To build up manufactures which could not be started if subjected to foreign competition. The effect of industrialization, according to Colin Clark,[8] is always to increase living standards and so to promote more foreign trade. When agricultural na-

---

7. *The Twenty Year Crisis.*
8. *Conditions of Economic Progress,* Macmillan, London, 1940.

tions build factories, national income rises, and then people buy more goods from abroad. They are *different* goods, but the volume is greater. If factories cannot get under way without protection of "infant industries," it follows that *tariffs increase trade, under certain circumstances.*[9]

2. To maintain industries after they are established, lest unemployment follow abolition of tariffs. True, this situation would theoretically right itself in the long run, but for the short run there would be acute suffering and deprivation, which no government likes to be responsible for.

3. To maintain war industries and strategic raw materials, in an uncertain world. Even Adam Smith made this exception. It has furnished the major drive for economic self-sufficiency in recent years. The United States can be expected to maintain its synthetic rubber industry for this reason, whatever the comparative cost of rubber from Malaya.

4. To provide revenue. It may not be easy to find other sources when customs duties are abolished. This is not an important reason for the United States.

5. To avoid having foreign goods dumped within one's borders, after foreign currencies collapse. At this very moment, most currencies in Europe seem to be collapsing.

6. To avoid such evils as the "depressed areas" in Britain, when she ceased to be the workshop of the world. Empty textile mills, deserted coalpits, decaying shipyards, the terrible misery of the Black Country, cursed England from 1920 to 1939. Read

9. L. R. Edminster of the U. S. Tariff Commission notes in the *Papers and Proceedings* of the American Economic Association, January 1943, that tariffs no doubt hastened industrialization. Meanwhile it is obvious that industrialization did not prevent but helped the growth of world trade during the past century. When protection is overdone, however, it can have a retarding effect.

J. B. Priestley's *English Journey,* if you are strong enough to stand it.

7. To avoid the deadening effect of a single industry. One-crop countries are no more to be desired than one-crop men. National strength and vigor comes from diversity of occupations, even if it does cost more. Under pure free trade, such diversity is not allowed, or it is achieved much more slowly. Goods must be produced where they are the cheapest, let the robots fall where they may.

Could We Fill Britain's Shoes?

One final point. The United States, as we have seen, is now a powerhouse relatively as great as was Britain a century ago. Why cannot we do what she did, and singlehandedly promote free trade and the gold standard? There are at least three pretty good reasons why not:

1. Americans lack the background for the role, a background which seafaring Britons had, together with colonies all over the world. Because we are an integrated country, with agriculture and industry well balanced, we lack the incentive Britain had. Also our high-tariff vested interests are extremely well entrenched.

2. Russia, to say nothing of France, Britain, and other countries, might strenuously object to such a unilateral system.

3. No such rate of expansion prevails as during the nineteenth century. Without the most careful planning, the postwar world is going to be plagued with surpluses.

Perhaps the nations must work the problem out together on a new formula, of which the Bretton Woods proposals are an encouraging beginning. Perhaps the nineteenth century was not quite such a Utopia as we have been taught to believe. Even if it was, history does not run backward.

5
THE TWENTIES

THE FIRST LARGE automatic factory on earth went into production in Milwaukee soon after the end of World War I. It took sheets of steel at one end of a huge hall, and in an uproar like a tank battle, delivered finished automobile frames at the other end.

The war had revealed a new dimension in mass production, a whole new level of possible output. For those with eyes to see, the end of poverty was at hand. By the same token, an economy of abundance, where production outran purchasing power, promised chronic surplus trouble, chronic depression and unemployment, unless the mechanisms of distribution were geared to the increased output of the machine.

Despite the British slogan of "business as usual," the war bent business completely out of shape. Trade, both internal and external, was largely taken out of the hands of private traders, to be planned and directed by the army and the government. It was not the total war of 1945, but it was a good 50 per cent war, far more universal than anything theretofore known.

One by one the Victorian commercial standards were set aside. The gold standard was everywhere abandoned, to be replaced by deliberately managed currencies. What was left of the world free market disappeared in a great structure of quotas, priorities, licenses, and requisitions. The freedom of the seas was repeatedly violated by both Germany and Britain. President Wilson was protesting the seizure of ships by the British before he began writing angry notes to the Wilhelmstrasse about U-boat outrages. Toward the end of the war, the Supreme Economic Council of the Allies was apportioning the raw materials of half the world. Six great Allied powers bowed before its planetary decrees — Britain, Russia, France, the United States, Italy and Japan.

New political and economic institutions, as well as new military and industrial techniques, were being rapidly developed by both belligerents. Tanks, fighting planes, Zeppelins, machine guns, Big Berthas, U-boats, the convoy system, the Food Administration, War Industries Boards — the world was on the march. Human ingenuity was in one of its most dynamic as well as destructive phases.

Versailles

President Wilson, armed with his Fourteen Points and a great fund of idealism, crossed the ocean to help write the peace of Versailles. If the League of Nations will not work by itself, he said, we must make it work. Hopes ran high.

The peace was signed — though it was not quite the peace which Mr. Wilson wanted. With considerable relief the victors officially scrapped their new political, military and economic institutions, and tried to turn back to the nineteenth century. Clemenceau, the Tiger, had been born in 1841. In military matters, progress ceased as abruptly as it had begun. In political matters, the principles of the French Revolution of 1793 were good enough. In economic matters, laissez faire and the world free market were to be restored without delay.

A curious thing happened. Most of the victors became static

and soft; the vanquished continued dynamic and destructive. Russia, in effect a defeated nation, also seemed to gain strength from her defeat. Later the Japanese joined the ranks of the dissatisfied powers.

The outstanding fact to grasp about the 1920's was that all right-thinking men directed their minds, and, where possible, their actions, to the prewar era. But stubborn as were their beliefs, and hard as they tried, *they could not get back.* The external situation was too much for them.

The outstanding fact to grasp about the 1930's was that after the Wall Street smash, the explosion of the Kredit Anstalt in Vienna, the gold crisis of 1931, many national leaders reluctantly concluded that the road back was closed, and turned to new experiments, new deals, and new orders.

The Old Men

One young British scholar fought through the war and came out of it a kind of mystical Galahad, as Lawrence of Arabia. In *The Seven Pillars of Wisdom* he said:

When we achieved, and the new world dawned, the old men came out again and took from us our victory, and remade it in the likeness of the former world they knew. Youth could win, but had not learned to keep, and was pitiably weak against age. We stammered that we had worked for a new heaven and a new earth, and they thanked us kindly, and made their peace.

E. H. Carr was not so old, but he was one of the architects of the treaty and was decorated for his part in it. Two decades later he was not proud of what he had done. In a less poetic way he came to agree with Lawrence, as have many careful students.[1]

1. In this chapter we will follow in a general way Carr's analysis of the 1920's, as set forth in his books *The Twenty Year Crisis* and *Conditions of Peace.*

France, Britain and the United States, says Carr, dictated the peace, and then sank into a mood of comfortable resignation. "Security and normalcy became the twin pillars of the temple. Both were interpreted in terms of the halcyon age before 1914." History was moving down a new road actually, but the elder statesmen were mentally committed to the old roads. So a gap opened between reality and ideology, which grew wider as the decade advanced.

In postwar Europe, planned economy, which rests on the assumption that no natural harmony of interests exists, and that interests must be harmonized by state action, became the practice, if not the theory, of every state. In the United States, the persistence of an expanding domestic market staved off this development till after 1929.

Military

The satisfied powers hoped for disarmament and lost interest in military progress. They built the Maginot line and broke General Billy Mitchell. "It is difficult," says Carr, "to exaggerate the advantage ultimately derived by Germany from the destruction of her armaments . . . a circumstance which obliged her not only to modernize her material, but to think out again from the start every problem of equipment and organization, while Britain and France remained embedded in the legacy of the past." (This makes one wonder, incidentally, what may happen after we destroy Germany's armaments for the second time.)

Self-Determination

On the political front a similar thing happened. Parliamentary democracy hardened in the nineteenth century pattern, with no attempt to adjust it to new conditions. Failing such adjustment, many democracies went to smash. Under Wilson's doctrine of self-determination, the peace treaty had set up a whole battery of shiny new democracies in Europe. Each proceeded to the creation of shiny new legislatures, executives, customhouses, armies, diplomatic corps, flags and national anthems. Each was endowed with exclusive national sovereignty. Yet the bombing plane and the high-power transmission line were already mocking at exclusive sovereignty in such cramped geographical quarters.

Said Secretary Lansing of Wilson: "When the President talks of self-determination, what unit has he in mind? Does he mean a race, a territorial unit, or a community? Without a definite unit which is practical, the application of the principle is dangerous to peace and stability." The definition given at Versailles was at variance with the trend of the twentieth century, which was in the direction of fewer and larger units.

Carr sums it up: "The liberal democracies scattered throughout the world by the peace settlements of 1919 were the product of abstract theory, struck no roots in the soil, and quickly shrivelled away." That was true in Poland, Latvia, Estonia, Lithuania, Yugoslavia; in Germany, Austria, and Turkey. I am not so sure about Czechoslovakia and Finland. I think they may have sent down some real democratic roots. But the roots could not hold when the high winds came.

Back to Laissez Faire

On the economic front, the story was repeated. The textile center of Britain announced a few months after the war: "Lancashire is perfectly sanguine of success once normal conditions have been restored." The idea was to sit back and wait for events to right themselves and then do business in the traditional way. But normal conditions never were restored, and Lancashire rotted on the dole for twenty years.

In both belligerent and neutral countries, industry and agriculture had been artificially stimulated by the war, in order to compensate for goods cut off, or to speed munitions. After the war, each nation struggled to maintain the expanded output on which jobs depended. War damage, except in Northern France, was repaired in a remarkably short time. The biggest bomb dropped weighed only 100 pounds. The new nations, created at Versailles, charged into the world market, competitors for the first time. In China, India, Japan, Latin America, new factories appeared, manned by workers who could exist apparently on crumbs, like the sparrows of the field. Japan in particular became a huge exporter of cheap textiles, toys and other goods, bringing grief to Lancashire.

Yet with all this new capacity to produce around the world, there were few more open spaces to exploit. The rate of population growth was leveling off, and quotas were damming up the natural flow of migration. The attempt to revert to nineteenth century methods in this changed structure, we can now see, was naïve. The louder the elder statesmen exhorted, the faster the workaday world drifted in the contrary direction — away from free trade, away from gold, away from the idea that each nation should produce only what it could do most cheaply.

Economic Nationalism

One began to hear a new word, "autarchy" (the Germans spelled it with a k). It referred to a drive for substitutes, synthetics and self-sufficiency, and was a synonym for economic nationalism. Mussolini was trying to force Italy to grow her own wheat. The Russian Five Year Plans were directed toward a closed economy. The Germans began to produce practically everything from a lump of coal — even butter.

When free trade was at its zenith, from 1850 to 1880, markets were expanding so fast that competition was relatively mild. Now in the 1920's, competition was becoming lethal. Many prices fell headlong as surpluses accumulated. Business firms were ruined. Commodities were dumped and burned to keep them from swamping the market. Traders bawled to high heaven. Governments intervened to help their businessmen. This meant subsidies, or restrictions on competitors' goods — and so poison to laissez faire. Cartels were another remedy. Big private interests got together to restrict world output and keep prices in line. Often governments helped them, or joined them.[2]

There was a League of Nations functioning, but it could stop nothing save very small wars. "The metaphysicians of Geneva," says Carr, "found it difficult to believe that an accumulation of ingenious texts prohibiting war was not a barrier against war itself." Non-metaphysicians, however, readily believed in the next war, and were alarmed about what would happen to their country when essential imports — food, oil, chemicals — should be cut off. Governments took steps to forestall this disaster, and their steps meant more control of foreign trade, more economic nationalism, and more fetters on the free market.

The New Banker for the World

The war had retired London as the financial center of the planet and turned the role over to Wall Street. The United States had also moved into Britain's place as the chief workshop of the world. Our national income in 1929 surpassed that of all the twenty-six nations of Europe put together. We were the world's largest single exporter, and second largest importer. We were the chief source of international investment funds, supplying more

2. These procedures were accentuated in the 1930's.

capital than Britain, France, Holland, and all other creditor nations combined. In 1927, Wall Street financed two billions of foreign loans. This was the peak. After 1929, lending abroad dried up to a miserable trickle.

As the leading creditor nation, we were supposed to lend capital abroad and take in enough imports to meet interest charges, so that foreign loans would not suddenly dry up. Britain had operated on such a formula for a hundred and fifty years. Americans loaned the capital all right, for a while, but by raising tariffs in 1921, 1922 and 1930, Congress made it impossible to take enough imports to balance the international books.[3]

America has been severely criticized for her so-called international irresponsibility during this period. But there was a mitigating circumstance which should be mentioned. America, a continental hunk of 3,000,000 square miles, was not Britain, an island kingdom of 94,000 square miles, badly needing imports of food for her people and raw materials for her factories. United States import needs in 1920 were relatively far less. We could feed ourselves, and had many industrial raw materials at home.

High Pressure

The excursion of Wall Street into international finance had both its hilarious and its tragic moments. Some day a competent historian will make rich and entertaining reading out of this brief episode. It was of a piece with other prime exhibits of the New Era — the leaping skyscrapers, Florida swamp lots, wild oil booms, flagpole sitters, the astronomical stock market.

The international books were temporarily balanced by selling foreign bonds and stock to innocents throughout the land. An investment house in New York would brief its shock troops as

3. Look again at the table on page 11.

new issues of foreign debentures, elegantly engraved, came out of the mill. Sometimes the investment house forced a reluctant foreign government to borrow so the house would have more merchandise to sell. The shock troops had both basic training in a special bond-selling school and commando work in the field. They descended on anybody who was reputed to have money, with irresistible dispatch and effrontery.

One of their number has since confessed his sins.[4] He was manager of a branch office in the South. His boss for a time was one of the lords of creation, the whitest of the white-headed boys of Wall Street. The author gives us a sample of a typical communiqué from headquarters:

> I should hate to think there is any man in our sales crowd who would confess to his inability to sell at least some of any issue of either bonds or preferred stocks that we think good enough to offer.
> We sent a long flash this week on specific issues, including Cuban Dominican Sugar bonds and Willys Overland Preferred.
> I have before me an analysis of individuals' sales on the issues included in the special premium commission arrangement. Mr. A's sales have been $29,700. We are very confident that he can give us better results on these issues. Mr. B has not responded, and has sold of Willys Overland only $1,000, and of Cuban Sugar none.
> Please give this question of the value of the work being done by the men in your office your most thorough study, and be sure that each man is definitely progressing.

Which meant, says our hero, to fire those troopers who did not come across with orders. Another flash:

> We are enclosing a revised description of some of our sugar issues which serves to illustrate the tremendous improvement in the bonds. . . . May we count on you to give us your full support . . . to estab-

4. *Scapegoat,* privately printed by Julian Sherrod, Dallas, 1931.

lish these bonds in the minds of the investing public as sound, safe investments, and as extremely attractive whenever purchasable on a 7% basis.

Before many months were out, these "sugar issues" were in default, and thousands of small investors had been knocked cold. Says our renegade: "I do not know why these 'creations' were created. We had to sell them. We sold them to friends. Taking the amounts now outstanding, the sugar bonds show a loss of $25,-000,000."

One of his clients was an elderly school teacher, who fell ill and had to have a series of operations. She had put $462.50 of her savings into a Cuban Dominican Sugar $500 bond. When she desperately needed cash, it was selling for $7. Another client was a kindly old gentleman who closed out his business and invested the savings of a lifetime. He bought Cuban hotels which slid from 100 to 50, Chilean nitrates from 97½ to 30, Brazilian states from 87 to 40.

Our hero was constantly being reminded from Wall Street headquarters that it was up to him to accept "the responsibility we have as a creditor nation." The bank traded on that slogan — and took its commissions. Its "creations" included securities of Australia, Brazil, Peru, Chile, German Cities, Poland, Yugoslavia, Greece, Italy, Uruguay. "We covered all the territory."

Unbalancing the Books

Of the total loans made by Americans abroad during the 1920's, to both governments and private concerns, it has been estimated that $10 billion are forever gone. Thus up to 1930, and including the defaulted war debts, we sent abroad some $20 billion of goods and services for which there has been no stuff returned, and probably will never be.

Perhaps, as we observed earlier, the war debts should have been written off as an additional contribution to beating the Kaiser. The private debts, however, were something else. Promoted by red-hot Coney-Island methods, chiefly for the turnover profit which was in them, these Cuban Sugars and German Cities were cheerfully lied about and crammed down people's throats. Investors lost their capital. From an impersonal view, however, the score was not a complete blank. For six or seven years foreign investments offset savings at home, and helped to keep employment high. In the last analysis, investors were giving their money away to keep fellow Americans at work. But folks abroad received the goods which the fellow Americans had produced.

L. R. Edminster, of the U.S. Tariff Commission, reviews the decade.[5] It really seemed for a while, he says, that the United States had discovered a magic formula whereby a great creditor country could:

1. Severely check its imports by high tariffs.
2. Expand its exports.
3. Collect payments on foreign loans.

"For several years it was possible, by resort to new lending, to keep the inherent absurdity of this conglomeration of conflicting policies below the surface." But the magic formula ran out as the new lending ceased, and the great depression was brought that much closer.

Far from heading back to Utopia, as the elder statesmen hoped, the decade after the war headed into confusion and depression. The League of Nations met regularly, and one international con-

5. *Papers and Proceedings* of the American Economic Association, January 1943.

ference after another was called. Sentiments of the most exalted order were expressed, and the Kellogg peace pacts were signed by fifty-three nations. But the world continued on a wild, unprecedented course to an unknown end.

6

THE THIRTIES

In September 1930, Dr. Nicholas Murray Butler of Columbia predicted that Cobden's principles of free trade were to gain more influence and exert a "practical effect on public policy." Even while he spoke, the soupkitchen lines were lengthening and the world depression deepening. In that same year Congress passed the Smoot-Hawley tariff, perhaps the most anti-Cobden measure in United States history.

Britain was loaning Germany huge sums to keep her afloat from week to week. In the next year, 1931, Britain herself, as we have seen, was forced off the international gold standard. International bankers, like the Rothschilds and the Morgans, began to lose the position and power they had held since the days of the Medicis. Their role was taken by the state.

Copper fell from 24 cents a pound to 5 cents, and tin from 58 cents to 18. The Kredit Anstalt bank failed in Vienna, rocking the continent of Europe. President Hoover proposed a moratorium on the war reparations payments of the Germans.

Meanwhile Britain gave the Cobdenites another severe shock by levying the first comprehensive tariff since the Corn Laws were repealed. Worse still, at the Ottawa Conference with her Dominions, she set up a system of "imperial preferences," which put the Empire on an exclusive trading basis as compared with the rest of the world.

In 1933, the Reichstag was burned, presumably by order of Hitler. Presently he appointed Dr. Schacht to devise some novel and curious experiments in foreign commerce. The New Deal was inaugurated in America, with accent on domestic reform and little interest in foreign relations, save for the so-called "good neighbor policy." In 1936, France abandoned the international gold standard, taking Holland and Switzerland with her.

One world crisis followed another, like salvos of artillery. The rift between theory and practice became a yawning chasm. Armchair students of international affairs, says Carr, were agreed as to the policy which governments ought to follow. But governments "acted in a sense precisely contrary to this advice, and received the endorsement of public opinion at the polls."

The Great Dollar Shrinkage

As the United States net national income fell from $80 billion in 1929 to $40 billion in 1932, dollars paid out abroad shrank from $7 billion to $2.4 billion. This disrupted trade channels around the world. Our foreign trade meant relatively little to us compared with our huge domestic market, yet its effect on world markets was greater than that of any other country. Geoffrey Crowther, of the London *Economist,* draws a significant contrast: "America is self-sufficient in a high degree; Britain, in no degree at all. To America, foreign trade is a marginal source of wealth; to Britain, an absolute condition of existence. The American financial structure is built around the producer; the British, around the trader."[1]

The shortage of dollars induced a heavy drain on the gold re-

1. In the *Yale Review,* Winter 1945.

serves and the foreign exchange reserves of other countries. Their currencies were undermined, with serious effects on prices and production. Even when off the gold standard, nations ship gold, if they have any, to settle international balances. The standard, as we noted earlier, is not concerned with gold as a salable commodity, but with a fixed relationship between the currency unit and a given weight of gold.

Let us stop a moment and look thoughtfully again at the figures of shrinkage cited above. While United States national income was cut in half, export dollars fell two thirds. Can there be any doubt of the intimate relationship? When the country was prosperous in the 1920's, its foreign trade was large, in spite of tariff boosts, but when it fell into heavy depression, its foreign trade almost disappeared. Per contra, when national income began to climb from the depression lows of 1933, both exports and imports climbed too. There is a simple moral here which does not always get into the discussions. When trade falls off, we blame tariffs, embargoes, government meddling, all sorts of things. *But by far the most important factor in American foreign trade has been the level of income and employment at home.*[2]

Dubious Assumption

Herbert Feis points out again, as so many students have done before, that the classic doctrine of the world free market rested on the assumption of full employment of men and capital.[3] It was thought that idle savings, except for limited and exceptional periods, simply could not occur. In the nineteenth century, with its

2. See Maffry and Lary, *Foreign Trade after the War*, Bureau of Foreign and Domestic Commerce, Washington, October 1943.
3. *The Changing Pattern of International Economic Affairs*, Harper, New York, 1940.

great growth of population and markets, they could not indeed, and the theory of automatic balance had some justification.

In the years after World War I, however, idle men and idle money reached such proportions that the victims, including workers, businessmen and farmers, turned to their government for help. They made a great clamor. They protested that they could not wait for the bottom to be reached. Where was the bottom? Before the automatic turning point came, they might all be dead.

So governments in effect took over their respective economies. Some did it mildly, some vigorously; some with dictators, some with legislatures. Governments subsidized the unemployed, and sometimes put them to work making things which might be had cheaper abroad. *The work was more important than the cheapness.* As in World War I, money ceased to come first.

In 1932 a friend gave me a firsthand illustration of the human reason for this. In the New England shoe city of Brockton, he had seen a store window full of shoes from Czechoslovakia. Make no mistake, he said, they were fine shoes and cheap. Standing by the window, he looked down the street and saw a line of unemployed shoe workers in front of a soup kitchen. Make no mistake, they were fine men and women. . . . A time comes when a government must decide whether to sacrifice the fine shoes or the fine men. Furthermore, when all the costs of relief are reckoned in, the imported shoes may not be so cheap as they first seem.

Though our official policy from War I to War II was to resurrect the old order, the actions of both government and citizens repeatedly violated it. And so, says Mr. Feis, contemplating these sad goings-on from his post in the State Department, "when the tragic sequence takes its course, the light in the economist's study burns low. The pattern of international relationships that he has evolved, half from observing what they were in peaceful times, and half by dreaming of what they might be, becomes all dreaming."

London Economic Conference

The Economic Conference which met in London in 1933 made a last effort to get back on the tried-and-true path. Our cooperation had been heavily counted upon. Binding agreements were under discussion. Then, like a thunderclap in a blue sky, Mr. Roosevelt pulled out. The Conference broke up in confusion. Why did the President loose the thunder? Because he was afraid that binding international agreements would endanger his program for domestic recovery. The United States did not need world trade so much as it needed more jobs at home. There was a conflict between the two goals, if not for the long swing, certainly for the short, and the President had to choose. As I read the record of the interbellum period, I think Mr. Roosevelt was well advised — though it is too bad the advice was not registered earlier.

The Trade Agreements

Although Mr. Hull was associated with the New Deal, he was as orthodox as Richard Cobden in matters affecting foreign trade. From 1934 to 1939, he negotiated some thirty trading agreements with other countries, whereby the United States reduced its tariff rates on certain items in exchange for a complementary easing of barriers.

The record shows, however, that the total effect of the agreements was small. The repercussion on exports was more marked than on imports. "Hence," says Percy W. Bidwell of the Council on Foreign Relations, "they tended to aggravate rather than correct the distortions in our balance of payments."[4] What the bal-

4. *Papers and Proceedings* of the American Economic Association, January 1944.

ance needed was more imports. The agreements "have not accomplished a real reform in the American tariff, consequently their effect on foreign tariffs has also been limited." It remains to be seen whether the effects will be any less limited after the war.

Kentucky Gold

While the State Department, under Mr. Hull, was trying to restore the classical pattern, the Treasury across the street was wrenching it out of focus with an unprecedented gold-buying program. The program continued until the United States had sequestered more than two thirds of all the free gold in the world — i.e., gold available for shipment and not in jewelry stores. These purchases alone would have wrecked the international gold standard, if there had been any left to wreck.

Not all our gold hoard, but the bulk of it, is said to be in Fort Knox. People speak of it as "dug out of one hole in South Africa and put into another hole in Kentucky" . . . which is a significant statement in itself. We now joke about gold. Before 1933, people would no more joke about gold than about the national debt or the Constitution. A great symbol has obviously fallen. When we abandoned the gold clause for federal securities, Mr. Justice McReynolds cried: "The Constitution is gone, and I am filled with humiliation!"

The Peek table showed that from 1914 to 1933 only two billions net in gold had come in to America from abroad. Soon after, the deluge began and it continued until the total stock reached $23 billion. It came to settle balances due to the excess of exports over imports. It came for servicing loans abroad which were not in default. It came especially as "refugee capital," transfers by Europeans fearful of coming wars and revolutions.

When President Roosevelt raised the price of gold from $21

an ounce to $35, he set the stage for one of the greatest laboratory experiments in economic history. According to many monetary theorists, the act should have turned the price structure upside down. It did nothing of the kind. Domestic prices hardly moved. The experts lost the confidence of many trusting citizens. They had told us that gold determined prices. The experiment proved that the value of gold had nothing to do with the value of goods inside the United States.

Two important things did happen, however, as a result of the President's action. The Treasury's gold hoard was worth 70 per cent[5] more one second after the decree went into effect — thus giving the Treasury a wonderful great paper profit! Outside the country, the $35 price was a bonanza for gold-mining countries, like South Africa, enabling them to buy 70 per cent more United States goods with the same weight of gold. This bargain sale stimulated foreign trade for a considerable time.

The gold hoard was not helpful to the United States in terms of stuff for stuff. We cannot use it all for wedding rings and dental supplies. As a currency standard, its future is uncertain. For a large portion of the hoard, we shipped out goods made by Americans in the sweat of their brows. It looks now as if we had received little that was useful in return. This conclusion was emphasized when American gold mines were closed by the government during the war, and workers were directed to dig essential metals like copper or lead — something that went inside a B-29.

The gold purchase program of the thirties was not far different in its final economic effects from the defaulted war debts, and the defaulted private foreign loans of the twenties. All three violated the common-sense rule of stuff for stuff. The total value

5. The price of a troy ounce of gold was raised from $20.67 to $35, or 70 per cent. This left the dollar worth only 59 cents in gold.

of goods and services shipped out under the three projects was
between $30 and $40 billion.

Funny Money

Suppose you have a pocketful of dollar bills which you want
to spend along Main Street. You go into a drugstore, make a
purchase, and slap one down. The clerk looks at it and says:
"That's no good here, that's good only in the hardware store!"
So you fish around in your pocket until you find a dollar bill which
is good in a drugstore. While you are at it, you separate the bills
into hardware dollars, grocery dollars, hash house dollars and
barbershop dollars. . . .

It would be a funny pocketful, but no funnier than the foreign
currencies which were issued as Kentucky drained the world of
its accustomed means of international payment. Germany laid
on the counter "security" marks, "emigrant" marks, "travel"
marks and "Aski" marks, to name a few. The British had a regular
pound and a blocked pound.

Funny Business

Volumes have been written on the novel international experiments of the 1930's. We have time to list only a few of the preva-
lent devices. Some were brand new; some were old methods now
greatly overworked. All were carried on largely by governments.
The motive, as we said earlier, was to try to keep the domestic
economy afloat and to give employment. Bilateral agreements,
clearing agreements, special deals, took the place of the open
market where supply and demand had been the rule. Instead of
a multilateral system with private traders from all nations dealing
on a world market, we find governments making deals with one

another about the flow of goods. The deals may be direct, or conducted by central banks, or by government-sponsored cartels. All this was in violation of classical theory, but as Mr. Feis points out, the theory "underestimated the possible advantages to *some* countries, at *some* times, of forming *special* and perhaps *exclusive* economic connections." Certainly Germany derived great temporary benefits from special deals. Without them she could not have rearmed.

Thirty-five nations raised their tariffs in 1932, as if to counter the United States increase of 1930. Russia screwed notch after notch in her government monopoly of exports and imports. When a country as large as Russia completely abandons the free market, the market is bound to be affected. Russia became a shrewd dumper of wheat on the world market. Other governments dumped too, meaning they sold surpluses abroad at a price lower than that which prevailed at home. If dumping on the market was out of the question, surpluses were sometimes dumped into the ocean, or burned. The Brazilian government burned mountains of coffee, year after year.

Canada embargoed pulpwood, Japan embargoed camphor. The French, Italian, Portuguese, and Japanese empires copied the British in arranging a line of "imperial preferences," where nationals were favored against foreign traders. Meanwhile the industrialization of Australia, India, China, Japan, Argentina, continued unabated.

Exports were licensed, subsidized, restricted by quotas. The woods — or better, the seven seas — were full of international cartels juggling the production and the price of copper, manganese, tin, steel. In those days cartels were fairly respectable. Even more respectable were commodity agreements, where governments in solemn conferences restricted world production of wheat, sugar and other crops.

"The practice of barter had already taken hold among the countries of eastern Europe after the war, who were desperately short of cash. Germany resolved it from an unrelated series of individual transactions to an organized national policy."[6] Sometimes barter was pure, as when Mexican oil was swapped for Italian rayon. Sometimes it had funny-money trimmings, being cleared through central banks, as when 1,500,000 crowns' worth of eggs laid by Hungarian hens were admitted to breakfast tables in Czechoslovakia on condition that Hungarian tourists would spend in Czechoslovakia the currency which the Czechs would need to pay for the eggs.[7]

Further to embarrass the free market, governments everywhere began to emphasize self-sufficiency. This hurt the wheat farmers, cotton growers, beef producers, of countries with long-established exports. Mussolini engineered the "battle of wheat" in an attempt to make Italy grow her own. France and Germany paid twice the world price or more to local wheat growers to increase acreage. Brazil built up a new cotton-growing industry.

Artificial fibers like rayon and nylon cut into established markets for cotton, wool and silk. The beneficiaries of the established markets called such material "ersatz," and tried to make it synonymous with shoddy. Sometimes it was, and sometimes it was a distinct improvement on the original. Autarchy was about the only coherent pattern which distinguished international commerce in the 1930's. Yet in one sense autarchy is the negation of commerce.

6. Douglas Miller, *You Can't Do Business with Hitler,* Little, Brown, Boston, 1940.
7. Cited by Feis in *The Changing Pattern.*

Reparations

Perhaps nothing illustrates the interbellum confusion better than the matter of German reparations — a fiasco which may profitably be reviewed in the light of the new reparations demands lately handed down from Potsdam. A scholarly study made by Stephen Spencer[8] summarizes the whole situation. It shows clearly that the victors, except Russia, cannot take reparations in any quantity without either ruining themselves, or revising their foreign trade policies of the thirties.

In 1921 the Paris Decisions had fixed German obligations at 226 billion gold marks (about $56 billion), to be paid in forty-two annual installments. Some reparations were to be made in kind — coal, labor, locomotives. But within the year it was found that the money total was too astronomical to make sense, and the principal was reduced to 132 billion marks. At the same time the London Ultimatum sternly decreed that if Germany did not honor the revised schedule, French troops would occupy the Ruhr. A few months later the troops marched in. The occupation reduced Germany's industrial output, and made it still harder to pay. A flight from the mark followed, and the famous runaway price inflation. When the situation was finally stabilized, the new mark exchanged for the old at the rate of one to one billion!

In 1924 the Dawes Plan was drafted; in 1928 the Young Plan. The former fixed no total, but the latter made a further reduction to 121 billion marks, and the period of payment was raised to fifty-nine years. No sooner was this plan agreed to, than the Wall Street crash knocked it galley west. In 1931 President Hoover was forced to declare a moratorium. *The next year the Lausanne Conference reduced the total due from Germany to 3 billion*

8. *The Antioch Review*, Summer 1945.

marks — or about one-seventy-fifth of the original total! But even this small change was almost immediately forgotten. All in all, Germany paid 11 billion marks on reparations account from 1924 to 1931. But at the same time she received from the victors 18 billion marks in loans. Mr. Spencer said:

Whatever may have been Germany's intentions about honoring its debts, it was effectively prevented by its creditors from making payment. Instead of receiving Germany's exports, its creditors took measures to exclude them, and all the while made efforts to facilitate an increase in its imports. . . . The trade policy following the war was the kind that might have been followed had the Allies been defeated and required to pay reparations to Germany.

As we saw in Chapter 2, money has little meaning in foreign trade except as a bookkeeping convenience. Germany could not pay her debts in marks, but only in goods. If she achieved an export surplus, she could take the dollars, francs and pounds, and reduce her debts. But every nation on earth fought against her achieving an export surplus, fought against taking German goods. Worse, they tried to force *their* goods on Germany, and give her an *import* surplus. Those high-pressure tactics of Wall Street banking houses, which we reviewed in the last chapter, were designed for precisely this end: to force loans, and thus American exports, on Germany.

So the whole reparations program became a roaring farce, where it was not a painful boomerang. Germany got more stuff than the victors, on net balance; nor was this due to any Machiavellian scheming on Germany's part. The victors would not take her stuff if they could possibly avoid it.

When the United States was supposed to absorb German imports, or their equivalents in triangular trade, Congress set up the highest tariff wall in history to block off imports. When Germany tried to send laborers into France to repair devastated areas as per agreement, French workers protested violently, saying their jobs were being stolen and their pay scales undermined. When the Reich tried to send coal to Italy under reparations, British coal operators and miners forced the British government to wrest from the Italian government an agreement to buy millions of tons of English coal *in place of free German coal!* . . . This, I think, is my favorite Alice in Wonderland story in foreign commerce.

Except for Britain's brief tryst with free trade in the nineteenth century, the nations of the world have been opposed to swapping goods and services. They like exports well enough, but they loathe imports — or better, powerful local groups make such a row that imports become politically impossible. The aversion is made the worse by the steady increase in price rigidities, monopolies and trade unions. Reparations can only be paid in goods, but free goods on the dock, like government surplus stocks from war, frighten the daylights out of local producers, who would rather dump the goods in the sea, lest prices be driven down. It is all very human, and all very crazy. It happened after the last war, and might happen again.

Today Russia is probably the only nation which can take reparations from Germany in a big way — assuming of course that bombed German industry is capable of an export surplus. There are no organized pressure groups in Russia to protest, and the goods can smoothly enter according to plan.

All this raises a fundamental point in foreign commerce. If the world is really to benefit from the exchange of goods and services, trade must either be much more free than in 1939, or much better planned by government export-import controls.

End of the Armistice

Late in 1930, Lord Cecil told the League of Nations that "there has scarcely ever been a period in the world's history when war seems less likely than it does at present." And then:

> In 1931 Japan invaded Manchuria.
> In 1935 Mussolini attacked Ethiopia.
> In 1936 the Spanish Civil War became a prelude to world war.
> In 1937 Japan invaded North China.
> In 1939 the Germans hurled their panzers into Poland.

Lord Cecil was apparently no better prophet than Dr. Butler. The whole decade was overshadowed with war. The fear of it was a major force in breaking up accredited trade customs. As one after another of the great powers was drawn into the conflict, international trade as such became a museum piece. In the next chapter we will examine what took its place.

7

TOTAL WAR

N o sooner did the first bombs crash in Poland than the United States lost all its trade with Germany, Scandinavia, the Low Countries and France. American vessels were barred by law from danger zones. Presently Mediterranean traffic closed up. Our trade with Continental Europe, which had been running at the rate of $700,000,000 a year, was virtually wiped out.

Commerce continued with Great Britain, the Empire, the Far East, South America; but its character began to change drastically. Our normal exports of tobacco, cotton, corn, were cut. Steel, copper, chemicals, aircraft and other war supplies shot up. To save farmers from disaster, the government had to move in with additional loans against crops which no longer could be exported.

After Pearl Harbor home industry rose to the highest levels ever known. Imports were limited by the loss of former sources of supply, as in Malayan rubber; by lack of shipping space; by government fiat. Practically nothing could be imported from anywhere without specific authorization from the War Production Board, working in conjunction with the Board of Economic Warfare.

Meanwhile shipments abroad were no longer restricted by the volume of dollars available in foreign hands. Our allies did not need dollars to obtain goods; all they needed were needs. From certain countries imports continued to come in — such as coffee from Brazil and mica from India, but we could ship little stuff in exchange. "Preclusive buying" by the Board of Economic Warfare was responsible for a considerable volume of imports — goods we did not particularly want, but which our enemies did.

The Bureau of Foreign and Domestic Commerce sums it up: "Foreign trade during the war has become in the main an integral part of the services of supply of the United Nations. The principal limitations are not a lack of demand, which is virtually insatiable, nor a shortage of dollar exchange. They are rather the physical limitations on productive and carrying capacity."[1]

In respect to what once were "exports," the government asked:[2]

Can we spare them from defense?
Can we exchange them for something we need for our defense?
Will they go to friend or foe?

In respect to what used to be "imports," the government asked:

Do they contribute to our military strength, including essential civilian needs?
Are we buying from countries whose production we want to encourage — such as Latin America?
Will the dollars we pay for them get into enemy hands?
Can we keep the goods out of enemy hands by buying them first?

Machinery

Catherine the Great, when asked what were the three most important requirements for making war, replied: "Gold, more gold, and still more gold."

1. Maffry and Lary, *op. cit.*   2. Following Herbert Feis.

The world has moved a long way since the Rothschilds and the Fuggers furnished the sinews of war to empresses and kings. The reply of any modern statesman would be: "Stuff, more stuff, and still more stuff." To get out the stuff requires centralized planning. Every belligerent, and most non-belligerents (ask the Swiss and the Swedes) set up elaborate agencies to move munitions, or to provide civilians with the essentials of life.

As an example, take the four Combined Boards:

Combined Production and Resources Board
Combined Food Board
Combined Raw Materials Board
Combined Shipping Adjustment Board

These were empowered by Churchill and Roosevelt in 1942 to merge the resources of the United States and the United Kingdom, coordinating them into a single program. The Boards were instructed to allocate munitions and ships as the strategy of the Combined Chiefs of Staff should require. Subcommittees were set up as needed for machine tools, medical supplies, tires and tubes, pulp and paper, and so on. Other members of the United Nations cooperated, through special contracts for special items, or through protocol agreements, as in the case of deliveries to Russia. A substantial part of the critical raw materials outside German and Japanese control were allocated to United Nations war industries through these planetary boards.

Again, the United States has merged its economy with that of Canada to an astonishing and little-publicized degree. The Alcan highway to Alaska is but one of many joint projects. It is not going to be easy to tear the two economies apart after the thorough welding job which has been done.

The War Balance Sheet

By 1944 the United States was sending to other countries, exclusive of supplies to its own armed forces, some $14 billion of goods a year, and getting back about $8 billion.[3] Of the total sent out, about $7 billion was for cash, the rest on Lend-Lease account. Thus the United States has, for the first time since 1914, an "unfavorable" balance of trade, in that it is paying out more dollars for imports than it is getting back for exports. On the basis of stuff for stuff, however, it is the same old thirty-year *unfavorable* balance. As usual, we are sending out more goods than we are getting back.

The excess of dollars going out has reduced the gold hoard from $23 billion in October 1941 to $21 billion in late 1944, and it is still declining. Meanwhile the Federal Reserve Board finds that foreign governments and central banks hold $17 billion in dollar credits and in gold, an increase of $7 billion in the last three years. Here is Brazil, which had a $50 million balance in 1940, and now has $295 million salted down. Brazil goes right on selling us coffee, but we cannot send Brazil nearly all the stuff she wants in exchange, so she takes dollar credits, or gold, or both. This is happening widely around the world. It should furnish a substantial reserve of foreign purchasing power after the war.

Foreign trade controls in the United States became inevitable after the fall of France in 1940. One by one they moved in to displace the private trader and prevailing methods. Here are some of the control devices:

  · Freezing foreign funds.
    Trade licenses for both exports and imports.
    Blacklisting Axis agents.

3. Federal Reserve Board, November 1944.

Stockpiling essential raw materials.

Preclusive buying.

Shipping priorities, and then —

Lend-Lease, to bring an entirely new principle into the international exchange of goods and services.

LEND-LEASE

By far the most significant effect on world trade is created by the Lend-Lease program. Already more than $41 billion worth of goods and services have been sent abroad on this account. For them we are getting no credits, no IOU's, no dollars, and relatively little tangible stuff. What are we getting? All the little Calvin Coolidges in the land are asking or getting ready to ask this question.

To answer it, one must leave the field of contracts and bookkeeping and enter the field of moral obligations. Lend-Lease is something to drive a C.P.A. quite mad. But to the philosopher it is perfectly plain. *Lend-Lease is not a pecuniary proposition.*

Its chief architect, Mr. Roosevelt, expressed its philosophy in these words. They are from the seventeenth report to Congress in November 1944:

We are not lending money under Lend-Lease. We are not receiving payments on account under Reverse Lend-Lease. The Lend-Lease system is, instead, a system of combined war supply whose sole purpose is to make the most effective use against the enemy of the combined resources of the United Nations, regardless of the origin of the supplies, or which of us uses them against the enemy.

More simply one might say: *From each according to his abilities; to each according to his needs.* Think of the United Nations as one community acting in concert against the Axis. Every part of the community does its best. Here crops are speeded for the war effort, there munitions are made, yonder the conscription of man power for combat divisions is exceptionally high. This area makes ships, and that one drives them through seas infested with enemy U-boats. Each area, each family, each man, puts his all into the United Nations pool of energy. The Combined Chiefs of Staff distribute the energy to the fighting fronts. What business have long-nosed bookkeepers in this total effort? It is a matter of men, materials, fire power, and survival.

Such seems to be the philosophy of Lend-Lease, and there is a great deal to be said for it. Russia contributed her man power, Britain her sea power, the United States her mass production facilities. The United States is by far the greatest "arsenal of democracy," but she is also by far the most sheltered from bombs. One house in every four in Britain is said to have been damaged or destroyed, while the destruction in Russia and Poland does not bear thinking about.

Again, the debts of World War I, we know now, were impossible to repay. Much hard feeling and recrimination, many cries of "Uncle Shylock" would have been averted had they never got into the hands of the bookkeepers. Lend-Lease was an instrument designed to keep this blunder from being repeated.

The Size of Lend-Lease

The theory is fine, but practice is encountering difficulties. To begin with, the bookkeepers have got hold of it and sought to measure it in dollars. The figures will be drilled into the American consciousness, which is dollar-minded, and will be exceedingly difficult to expunge. Perhaps I should not do it, but I am just enough dollar-minded myself to give the latest summaries.

From March 11, 1941, when Lend-Lease was first invented,

to May 31, 1945, goods and services valued at $41,208,000,000
were shipped to our allies as follows:[4]

Great Britain	$29,000,000,000
Russia	10,000,000,000
France	510,000,000
China	362,000,000
American republics	336,000,000
Other nations	1,000,000,000
Total	$41,208,000,000

Against this the bookkeepers had recorded $5,500,000,000 of
reverse Lend-Lease, primarily in the form of billeting our troops
abroad.

So that leaves them owing us $36 billion, does it not? . . .
Wrong: utterly, completely and hopelessly wrong! You have not
counted in the twenty million dead in Russia, or the wreckage of
London, Liverpool and Coventry. How are you going to value
that? If the philosophy as stated above is valid, our allies owe us
nothing, and these figures mean almost nothing.

A breakdown of the totals means something, however, in so far
as it gives us an idea of the *kind* of stuff we have contributed to
the pool. Thus about 54 per cent of all has been munitions, with
aircraft the largest item; 21 per cent has been industrial materials like steel, 13 per cent farm products, 12 per cent services,
including repair of ships, ferrying of aircraft, and the like.

A Gold Mine for Demagogues

Lend-Lease could easily create a debt problem the way the records are now reported. Instead of a $10 billion problem, how-
ever, as in 1918, it might be $50 billion this time. "In the whole

4. Leo Crowley's report in *The New York Times*, August 22, 1945, as Lend-
Lease to Britain was halted.

field of the sharing of war burdens," says Eugene Staley, "two things have to be avoided like the plague: legal ideas and accounting ideas."[5] Are we pooling our resources in a common effort, or are we making a good thing out of selling supplies? If General MacArthur turns over an American tank to Australian troops, should we charge them for the tank, or should they charge us for the crew? How do you price the crew? "The whole practice of reciprocal Lend-Lease bristles with political dangers." It comes uncomfortably close to that atrocity myth of World War I, in which the United States was supposed to pay France "rent for the trenches."

The present Lend-Lease records are a gold mine for demagogues. Wipe them out! says Staley. Keep no dollar records at all, especially no reverse computations. Keep *inventory* records of physical transfers, but do not price the items. Turn inventory balances over to UNRRA when the war is over.

In the discussion of Mr. Staley's paper, Mr. A. F. W. Plumtree of Canada noted that cash, credit and gifts were all familiar devices in exchange for goods, but Lend-Lease introduces a "fourth and novel basis of international trade — an uncertain obligation, to be assessed by an unknown person, on an unspecified day of judgment." Nothing could better show the folly of trying to put Lend-Lease in the frame of reference of commercial trading. *It simply is not that kind of animal.*

What kind of animal is it? The joint pooling concept is the only one which makes sense to me. From each according to his abilities. . . . But this concept rapidly loses its force when the fighting stops. There is not much point to a philosophy of joint sacrifice when the shooting and the dying end. Relief and reconstruc-

5. *Papers and Proceedings* of the American Economic Association, January 1943.

tion cannot be put on a strict commercial basis either, but the philosophy is different from wartime Lend-Lease. The guns are silent, and blood has ceased to flow. President Truman halted Lend-Lease as Japan surrendered.

There should be no net debt left when Lend-Lease terminates. If the national interest of the United States demanded that Britain and Russia and China be kept in the war, then Lend-Lease was the most sensible way to do it. We got as much out of it as did our allies, and probably at a smaller sacrifice. Criticism should not run in terms of financial liability, but only of the strategy of disposal, and the efficiency of administration, together with the most careful investigation of any alleged cases of resale of lend-leased goods. If we have gone above the commercial level in this matter, our allies must certainly meet us on that plane.

Dilemma of Britain

Before Lend-Lease, Britain had paid us more than $3 billion for munitions, cash on the barrelhead. This had exhausted all her investments in the United States. If Lend-Lease had not come along, Britain would have gone under in 1941 — or so a great many qualified observers believe.

There is a legal provision that not only forbids Britain to use Lend-Lease supplies for resale as exports, but, to quote the *Economist*,[6] "forbids the export of wholly British products similar to those received under Lend-Lease, and puts the revival of the export trade at an intolerable disadvantage." These are strong words. At the same time, any American can see it would be intolerable to ship Diesel engines for the war pool, which the British might turn around and sell to Venezuela. But how shall we fairly judge a trace of Lend-Lease in a British export? Say the

6. November 11, 1944.

Diesel engine is wholly made in Britain, but contains a few ounces of copper that originally arrived on Lend-Lease? Suppose, at the same time, our Diesel manufacturers cannot get priorities for copper to fill Venezuelan orders? This kind of situation has already produced some acute headaches on both sides of the water.

Englishmen are deeply disturbed, and desperately want to get the matter straight. They are in agreement with Hitler on one pronouncement at least: "Export or die!" Let us examine the view of Geoffrey Crowther, on what our chief ally faces when the war is over.[7] In deciding about traces of copper we should keep this view in mind.

Export or Die

Britain is a small, tightly packed island, poor in natural resources, rich in capital. The United States is a loosely settled continental slab, with tremendous resources. The war, accordingly, has had quite different economic effects on the two nations. Mr. Crowther makes the following comparison:

	Source of War Output	
	In United States	In Britain
	Per Cent	
Increased production	100	41
Decreased consumption	−14	29
Drafts on capital	14	30
Total war output	100	100

Thus the United States has fought the war out of new production primarily. We increased butter along with guns, and drained capital only to the extent of the extra butter.

Britain, on the other hand, has fought the war primarily by

7. *Yale Review,* Winter 1945.

tightening her belt, and drawing on her stock of capital. We have come out of the war stronger than ever. Britain has come out of it gravely weakened.

Britain's prewar trade balance, averaged by Mr. Crowther, shows:

Imports, including invisible items		$4,700,000,000
Exports	$2,700,000,000	
Income from investments	1,000,000,000	
Income from shipping	550,000,000	
Income from banking, etc.	250,000,000	4,500,000,000
Deficit — capital shrinkage		$ 200,000,000

Even before the war Britain was eating into overseas investments to balance needed imports. But in 1944 the situation was infinitely worse.

Imports as above		$4,700,000,000
Exports estimated at	$700,000,000	
Invisibles estimated at	750,000,000	1,450,000,000
Deficit		$3,250,000,000

Imports, says Mr. Crowther, cannot be cut without depriving people of food, or factories of raw materials. Exports, not including munitions of war, have fallen to about a quarter of the prewar total, while invisible export items are off about 60 per cent. Every liquid investment abroad is said to have been sold. Long-term investment income is largely in default or frozen or run down — like the vast rubber plantations in Malaya. The greater part of the merchant marine is at the bottom of the ocean. Exchange controls by the several governments have shorn the London banking and insurance houses of much of their income.

The Only Solution

All this happens at a time when liquid reserves have been exhausted, leaving nothing to tide Britain over the transition period. *So the only solution, says Mr.* Crowther, *is to build up exports not only to prewar dimensions, but enough more to balance the vanished invisible items.* "This is a problem to which the United States has no parallel." It dominates British thinking day and night. It is the reason why English businessmen could not see eye to eye with Cordell Hull on free trade; why Eric Johnston's pleas for unencumbered private enterprise leave them cold. The British government must stay in the center of the picture, planning with business the restoration of Britain's wasted capital. It is a task to be reckoned in decades. On top of it is bomb damage replacement, which no private banker in his senses would touch without government guarantee.

In these circumstances, only the most fanatical Cobdenite would call for an immediate return to free international trading. "To attempt to do the work by the method of scramble would be to invite disaster," says Mr. Crowther, "there is no alternative to the method of priority, and priority involves a tight control." England, the mother of free trade, must now renounce it for the indefinite future.

Finally, Mr. Crowther makes a significant point. There is no struggle in Britain, he says, between government and business. One reason is the stark necessity of cooperation as shown in the above figures. Another is that the tories, the party of the businessmen, ran the government for twelve years up to 1945. "To regard the state . . . as the enemy of the people's liberty is in the American tradition, but not the British. On the contrary, the British state *is* the British people, and the people's creation cannot harm the people."

In Conclusion

The major effects of World War II on foreign commerce appear to be these:

1. Private trade and investment virtually disappeared in favor of government and supragovernment controls, aimed at winning the war. Even where private traders continued to operate they did so under strict priority and license.

2. The United States has developed a new invention in foreign commerce called Lend-Lease, which is neither leasing, lending nor commerce. Whatever it is, it saved Britain, saved Russia, and broke Hitler.

3. Britain, the home of Cobden and Bright, has had her foreign commerce ruined by the war, including her ships, foreign investments, export markets, services of banking and insurance. No responsible Englishman, to my knowledge, believes that she can find payments for the imports she so desperately needs, by anything less than rigorous economic planning. Her prewar exports must be increased at least 50 per cent to balance losses in other departments.

4. Self-sufficiency in the United States has been markedly advanced by the war. Consider synthetic rubber, the new plastics, the metal substitutes, the new crops. As we shall see, this does not necessarily decrease the total volume of foreign trade, but it will change its form.

5. The enormous destruction abroad of cities, homes, factories, farm lands, will require enormous amounts of capital goods to replace them. Much of this can come from local sources — brick, stone, cement, labor; much cannot.

6. Sweeping changes have occurred in the debtor-creditor status of nations. Canada, for instance, has already become a great creditor nation.

7. The currencies of some countries, like China and Greece, are rapidly going over the moon. A huge revaluation task lies ahead.

8. Finally, the war has sharpened the demand for new and improved methods in international commerce. If we needed them after the last war — as the whole interbellum history demonstrates that we did — how much more bitterly shall we need them after this one!

The international bank and the currency stabilization fund proposed at Bretton Woods are two inventions which may go a long way toward providing an answer.[8] They neither return us to the nineteenth century, nor plunge us once more into the bilateral deals of the twenties and thirties. Like Lend-Lease, they are something new in the world.

8. See Chapter 11, for discussion of Bretton Woods.

8

TRANSITION

THE TRANSITION FROM WAR to peace promises to be more complicated than ever before. This is the first total war the world has known, affecting the day-by-day habits of relatively more civilians. Once wars were the business of professional soldiers, the king and his money lenders; civilian life continued without much interruption for those who happened to live outside the fighting zone. Says H. G. Wells: "The total influence of the old warfare upon human destiny was enormously exaggerated by the nationalist historians. It was of infinitely less importance than migration. The peasant life went on unchangingly, squalid and laborious, as it had been going on for the majority of human beings since agriculture began."[1]

World War I broke up this continuity in many areas. Now it has been so shattered that European civilization may not be restored. Felix Morley, among others, believes that Europe may sink into a barbaric stupor for generations. He says:

To avoid a sharp spiritual let-down, and a reaction of intense cynicism, bitterness and isolation, it is essential that we should soon begin to study the map of Europe . . . as the ruined shell of an utterly exhausted — very possibly a dying — civilization. . . . Nobody is necessarily to blame for failure to reestablish something like normal con-

---

1. *The Shape of Things to Come*, Macmillan, New York, 1933.

ditions in districts whence the tide of battle has long receded. What is important is the evidence that restoration of normal conditions begins to seem beyond our power of accomplishment.[2]

If there is little health in Europe, the Far East presents no less dismal a picture. One's mind can hardly grasp the probable dislocation which will appear in China, Japan, Burma, India, the Dutch East Indies, as the curtain rings down in the Pacific theater. What Great Power is going to be responsible for half the population of the world concentrated in the Far East? On what basis? For how long?

"Conditions in Manila as I saw them," said Senator Tydings, "are beyond description. We found it almost completely wrecked, hardly a home habitable, without water, without transport, without food, and with almost nothing with which to look after a suffering population."[3] He told of 600,000 people in the city being fed by the U. S. Army. Conditions are so bad there can be no sugar crop for three years. Financial, administrative and living conditions "are in unbelievable confusion."

The Wreck of Europe

A Quaker welfare agency reported on Normandy in November 1944 after the fighting had ceased. "There is complete destitution everywhere. . . . Hundreds of thousands of people are without the barest essentials. They are cold, have nowhere to live, no blankets, no change of underwear, no shoes, no pots to do a little cooking even if they found somewhere to do it."[4] Out of 18,000

2. *Human Events,* February 7, 1945.
3. In *The New York Times,* June 5, 1945, after the Maryland Senator's return to Washington from the Philippines.
4. American Friends Service Committee, *Foreign Service Bulletin,* January 15, 1945.

homes in Le Havre, 14,000 were destroyed. In Caen, no water or gas supply, and electricity only an hour a day on certain days.

Europe is probably growing only about half its normal food supply. There is a tragic shortage of drugs, medical supplies, seeds, fertilizers, fodder, oils. Refugees are wandering aimlessly about the Continent, bombed out, starved out, with nothing left to live for. Serious epidemics may be gathering.

Factories and workshops lie in ruins from Brest to Warsaw; salt water has poisoned a million fertile acres in Holland; agriculture has been thrown out of its normal rhythm, where it is not altogether halted by devastated lands and by the lack of man power and equipment. Perhaps most serious of all are the shattered ports and docks, the wrecked railroads, bridges, switchyards, the blasted rolling stock, the empty canals.

Liberation meant much to the spirit of the people, but economically these nations were set further back. Imports ceased altogether. Each country had to live on its own resources. As raw materials were used up, especially coal, factories closed down. Inflation became a terrible menace as scarcities grew worse. With Allied armies in control, no local government could make any plans for the future.

The population of non-Russian Europe is, or was in 1939, around 380 million. No man, woman or child among these millions feels safe as the war ends. Most of them are hungry, and altogether too many disabled or sick. Who is going to help these 380 million people find some measure of security? By what methods? How long will it take? Their fathers did not find security after the last war. Fear never left the Continent after 1918; and in 1939 it became acute terror as the bomb bays opened. And now the atomic bomb has come.

Relief, Not Trade

Until Europe is growing food again, and manufacturing some of her own supplies, people will have to exist on relief. Russia may have some foodstuffs, Britain can do a little, but the bulk of it must come from the United States. If it does not come, millions will die of starvation next winter. In these circumstances it is meaningless to talk about "trade" with Europe — or with the Far East, for that matter. If we have the food to spare, we can help build the future peace of the world, and help Europe, by giving it away.

On what basis should we give relief to Europe? It cannot be given fairly without continental control of transport. No local government should be allowed to sequester freight cars, as was done in 1919, with people starving in the next valley. The armed forces of occupation, representing Britain, Russia, France and the United States, should keep the freight cars, the ships, the trucks, running as a unified continental system. These forces may have to get very tough with hoarders, monopolists and sequesterers.

The administration of relief and reconstruction can make or break the European economy for generations. There should be no discrimination against former enemies in dispensing food and medicine. An epidemic can start as readily on the Rhine as on the Seine. Both Hiram Motherwell[5] and Carr[6] insist that relief should be given to friend and foe alike. Any other policy of distribution is politically unworkable, for it is impossible to classify the political guilt or innocence of millions of individual children and other civilians, before giving them a meal. Where there is not enough to go around, of course friends in equal need should have priority over foes.

5. "Rebuilding Europe After Victory," Public Affairs Pamphlet No. 81, New York, 1943.
6. *Conditions of Peace.*

UNRRA

Forty-four of the United Nations joined together on November 9, 1943, at the White House in Washington, to form the United Nations Relief and Rehabilitation Administration. Each nation was to make available one per cent of its national income. For the United States that meant about $1,500,000,000. UNRRA is supposed to furnish not only food and medical supplies, but seeds, fertilizers, insecticides, tractors, to restore agriculture so that nations can feed themselves as soon as possible. It is supposed to repatriate displaced persons, notably the slave labor armies of the Nazis.

UNRRA is now operating in Europe, but on a limited scale, with a good deal of administrative difficulty. The Russians so far refuse to have its agents in their zone of influence; certain nations with gold reserves are too proud to stand in the bread line. The formula for effective relief has not yet been worked out.

It has been proposed that U. S. Army stocks in Europe, not earmarked for the Pacific, be released to UNRRA. This would accomplish three purposes — feed the hungry, prevent surpluses at home, save transportation.

Reconstruction

After relief will come reconstruction. It might be defined as the operations necessary to enable a community to support itself again — such as rebuilding ports, railroads, factories, highways, cities, houses, power lines, dams, turbines. Billions of man-hours have gone into the job of smashing up the capital equipment of Europe, and billions more will have to go into replacing it. There is said to be hardly a railroad bridge left in France; some districts are as remote from Paris as in the middle ages.

Sometimes one wonders: Is this to be the fate of Europe,

keeping people employed in a giant systole and diastole of tearing down and building up? Is this to be the fate of America also, to help demolish Europe every generation, then to try and build it up again? A disaster economy, world without end? . . .

Professor Carr proposed a European Planning Authority, to be set up by the Great Powers after victory is won, and the first relief needs satisfied, to direct reconstruction. It is still the most intelligent proposal I have seen for the transition period. Carefully worked out, it would not only put Europe in a position to carry on again, but might at the same time lay the basis for a continental federation, and so help the peace of the world. The bloody history of Europe, and its long supremacy in military science and materials, make it clear that there will be no peace on earth until Europeans can contrive to live together less violently.

The Authority, said Professor Carr, should control all transport facilities, direct the rebuilding of bombed areas, reconvert the major industries, such as coal, iron, chemicals, from war to peace. It was to establish credits for external trade, unify and stabilize European currencies, enforce a customs union inside Europe, and deal as a unit with the outside world.

It is probably too late to adopt Professor Carr's sensible program in detail. The world, and Europe, will be the losers. The Potsdam declaration seems to reduce Germany from the second greatest industrial nation on earth to a peasant economy. Germans may or may not deserve this, but every European will suffer with them, for it was German industry that kept the standard of living in Europe relatively high. Wipe it out, and unless it can be set up somewhere else, down goes all Europe. Where would the American standard of living be if Pittsburgh, Detroit, Cleveland, and all the industrial Northeast were wiped out?

Will Russia Do It?

"A shattered civilization," says Felix Morley,[7] "offers no economic alternative other than state control. With the growing military triumph of the Soviet Fatherland the movement of more people to the Communist bandwagon is automatic, needing no impetus from Moscow. It is not merely in the physical aspects of combat that the Soviet regime has proved itself extraordinarily competent. Unlike the British and American leaders, Stalin has consistently and intelligently regarded the actual fighting as a means to an end rather than an end in itself. . . . Of all the belligerents, we should remember, Russia has been the only one wise enough to concentrate all its energies on a single front."

As I write, Russia dominates Finland, Poland, the Baltic States, Austria, Czechoslovakia, Hungary, Rumania, Bulgaria, Yugoslavia, and a large and growing slice of Germany. She is laying down the law to Turkey and Persia. Her ambitions in Asia are unknown, but may include Manchuria, Korea and the communist-controlled provinces of China. Her troops are there.

Britain is apparently trying to set up a counter bloc in Europe, including France, the Low Countries, Scandinavia, Western Germany, Italy and Greece.

Whose will is the stronger? Who has superiority of fire power on the spot? Who knows best what he wants? Who can promise security and jobs to more people? Who best understands the revolutionary transition period in which the world now finds itself?

The democracies will have to work fast if Russia is not to set up a unilateral European federation. Political systems, like nature, abhor a vacuum. If we have nothing tangible to offer, the mass of Europeans in their agony may turn to Moscow. Will Rus-

7. *Loc. cit.*

sia perhaps succeed in doing what Napoleon and Hitler failed to do?

The Line Forms on the Left

The Bureau of Foreign and Domestic Commerce looks into the future and finds that the distribution of purchasing power among the several nations after the war will have little relation to the needs for relief, reconstruction, or commerce.[8] Therefore, it concludes, "rationing, allocations, price control and exchange restrictions must be continued during the interim period, if gross injustices, and possibly a disastrous boom-and-depression sequence . . . are to be avoided."

Foreign demand will compete with domestic demand for scarce supplies, and contribute, as it did in 1919, to the danger of inflation. Some Latin American countries, and a few others, will be able to finance purchases from swollen dollar balances. Brazil, as we noted in the last chapter, has increased her reserves of purchasing power abroad sevenfold. Holland and Belgium hold substantial balances in this country. "The problem in our trade with these countries will be to prevent dissipation of these reserves in an orgy of competitive bidding."

As everyone knows, the world production of automobiles has stood substantially at zero for nearly four years. It does not take great imagination to picture the demand when the first new models come off the conveyors. The line forms on the left! Nor does it take much imagination to picture the rage in Kansas City or San Francisco if Brazilians, Mexicans and South Africans outbid the home folks. Without a system of priorities we might see fighting in the streets!

As the war ends, governments of neutral countries as well

8. Maffry and Lary, *op. cit.*

as belligerents are in full control of each nation's foreign trade, shipments, exchanges and investments. All signs suggest that this situation will continue through the transition period. UNRRA is a planned operation, and so are the proposals for European reconstruction outlined above. Russia has had a state monopoly of foreign commerce for twenty-five years. The new French government is proposing state control of all exports and imports. Britain, as Mr. Crowther has warned us, can be expected to control her foreign commerce rigorously for years to come in an effort to close the gap between imports and exports. Britain is already signing trade pacts for government "bulk purchases" — i.e., the whole crop — with Canada, Australia and New Zealand. Now that the Labor government has come in, state controls will be tighter.

Conference at Rye

Businessmen of the world met at Rye, New York, in the fall of 1944 to discuss postwar problems. Conclusions may fairly be summarized as follows:

Foreign businessmen admire many of our products, especially trucks and machine tools. They will accept presents if the United States wants to play Santa Claus, but they would prefer to pay, if they are permitted to pay in due time. They can pay only in goods and services.

They are disturbed about our tremendous merchant fleet. Will we monopolize the world's shipping?

They are disturbed about our supremacy in the air.

They are disturbed about our tariffs. Will the walls stay so high that credits granted now cannot be liquidated by imports later? The recent extension of the Trade Agreements may allay their fears a little.

They are disturbed about unemployment in the United States after the war. Will we go into a tailspin and pull the world down with us?

Foreign businessmen at Rye said that their governments would, of course, control trade during the transition, and assumed that ours would follow suit. This made some American delegates a bit uncomfortable. The latter had hoped to steer the world in the direction of a more liberal program, with government interference at a minimum, and they said so. The foreign delegates listened politely.

1950 Balance

It is a rash man who will prophesy the American foreign trade balance in the transition period. Here is one prepared by the National Planning Association, and I give it for what it may be worth:[9]

Exports		$10,000,000,000
Invisible exports		600,000,000
Total		$10,600,000,000
Imports	$ 6,000,000,000	
Tourists abroad	600,000,000	
Remittances abroad	200,000,000	
Government expenses abroad	100,000,000	
Total	$ 6,900,000,000	
Long term loans	3,000,000,000	
Short term loans	700,000,000	
Total	$10,600,000,000	

9. Pamphlet No. 37, Washington, 1945. See also Milo Perkins in *The Atlantic Monthly,* September 1945, for another postwar balance sheet of $10 billion exports.

So we balance out with 3.7 billions of loans, about a third of all. Will we ever take the imports to balance on a stuff for stuff basis, or will these loans go the way of the three Christmas tree programs before World War II? If the latter, as a citizen and a taxpayer I think I would rather make gifts, at least for short-term credits covering relief and reconstruction. It seems cleaner. There is hate enough in the world without encouraging the bitterness which flows from defaulted debts.

There is also a brighter side to the picture. Where our loans represent exports of *capital goods* — generators, locomotives, machine tools — and in so far as these permanently raise standards of living abroad, perhaps they will not be defaulted in the long run. As Professor Colin Clark has pointed out, more foreign factories do not necessarily destroy foreign markets — they may create them. The United States in the nineteenth century was a classical example. We were a "backward" agricultural country developed by foreign capital. "The result was not only a great and rapid expansion of our ability to buy the manufactured goods of our former creditors, but the creation of a new market for the goods of the world. Economic development creates good customers because it increases income and purchasing power."[10] *Loans which transform an agricultural nation into an industrial one* might avoid default and help everybody.

Not-So-Brave New World

Fortune, aware of the difficulties which confront American business in the transition period, has given an honest and revealing example.

In 1944 a high official felt the time had come to lift U. S. government restrictions on certain imported products. The acute shortages

10. National Planning Association, *op. cit.*

were over. He called a conference of leading importers and told them the government was going to get out of their business. At first they were enthusiastic. This was what they had been praying for. Then a question crossed their minds. One of their members asked:

"I suppose the government will go on buying abroad and let us take care of distribution?"

The high official shook his head. "No, gentlemen, my office is *really* getting out. You are going to handle the whole thing just as you used to do."

"You mean we have to dig up our old contacts abroad?"

"Yes."

"And fight for shipping space?"

"Yes."

"And finance the business ourselves?"

"I mean, gentlemen, that you are going to have to stop drawing fees while the government does the work. You are all going back to competition, enterprise, and profit and loss."

There was a profound silence. Finally the spokesman found his voice: "If that's the case, then for God's sake let's keep on with the rationing."

This, it seems to me, is the keynote of transition. Until the postwar world shakes down into some sort of order, and especially until the great Russian powerhouse comes into a calculable equilibrium, we ought to "keep on with the rationing." Carr thinks it might take twenty years. Let us hope he is overpessimistic. With the Bretton Woods program accepted all around, equilibrium might be won much sooner.

Of one thing we can be quite sure. The United States, with the best will in the world, cannot operate a multilateral world market by itself.

9

PROSPECTS FOR A WORLD
STATE

There is a tendency in some quarters to believe," says Geoffrey Crowther, "that economists have some formula which will absolve the politicians from working out solutions of the problems facing them. This is pure political escapism. The political must come first. . . . Unless reconstruction can take place within the framework of tolerable political security, the economic effort will be in vain."[1]

What manner of political core shall we assume for the whole world when the war is over? Without a fairly definite picture in mind, it is meaningless to discuss the probable course of international commerce for the long swing. Broadly speaking, there appear to be four theoretical alternatives for the political structure of the postwar world.

1. A genuine world state, possessing military power, to which all nations are subordinate.
2. An alliance of the victorious Great Powers, supporting with their separate armed forces a League of Nations and other international agencies.

1. *Papers and Proceedings* of the American Economic Association, January 1943.

3. The 1939 international structure, with several Great Powers, and some sixty minor powers, all claiming unrestricted sovereignty.

4. The 1870 international structure, where one great power policed the world, and free trade was at its zenith.

The world state, with a court and police force, is what many Americans have hoped would arise like a phoenix from the ashes of this war. Week after week, for instance, *The New Yorker* returns to the theme, and the editors of this highly sophisticated journal are not noted for their starry-eyed qualities. Thus on December 9, 1944: "Our belief is that the way lies through a federation of democratic countries, which differs from a league in that it has a legislature that can legislate, a judiciary that can judge, and an executive that can execute. It does not have to operate through diplomacy, and it has a No Fooling sign on the door. . . . You can't have your anarchical society and eat it too."

The American people seem to support *The New Yorker*. A Gallup Poll in 1944 showed 74 per cent in favor of a world police force.

The Idea of the World State

The parliament of man, the federation of the world, is an ancient concept. It underlies the great religions which hold that all men are brothers. The Roman Empire federated western civilization. The Roman Catholic Church exercised a political suzerainty in the middle ages. Poets and philosophers have acclaimed the world state since time out of mind. Its most eloquent and devoted proponent in recent years has been H. G. Wells.

The idea of a family of nations, sovereign and independent, each with its own army, navy, flag, national anthem, currency and courts, is something new as history goes. It came into Europe about 300 years ago.[2] The nation-state system corresponded with the breakup of feudalism, the Reformation, the fragmentation of the Holy Roman Empire. The Treaty of Westphalia in 1648 recognized the principle of self-determination for small nations. It ended the religious wars and made the "first great architectural blueprint of the European nation-state system."

International rules were first recognized during this period. They replaced the Church's uneasy control of secular princes. The balance of power principle emerged from the shifting political affinities of the time. Little states served as buffers between big ones.

In due course the advance of mechanized warfare caused little states to relax their military outlays. They saw it was hopeless to try and keep up with the Great Powers, and they sought security in *neutrality*. Sweden and Switzerland actually avoided World War II by a disciplined adherence to the principle, though the battle raged all around them. Switzerland, indeed, the home of the Red Cross, the Geneva Convention for the treatment of prisoners of war, the League of Nations, has a special status as a permanent neutral.

The Price of One World

All men of good will aspire to that one government in one world where war will be as illegal as a riot in Times Square, and as amenable to control by officers of the law. But not many men of good will have cared to see their problem in cold colors. To see it through prisms is to invite the fate which befell Woodrow Wilson.

2. See Bruce Hopper in *Foreign Affairs*, April 1945; also Charles A. Beard, *The Idea of National Interest*, Macmillan, New York, 1934.

The world state cannot be built out of stirring phrases, any more than war can be prevented by laying a fountain pen, with appropriate sentiments, to a Kellogg peace pact. There are certain cardinal points to get straight before one can begin to think usefully about the federation of the world. They are:

First, to be a functioning political organization and not a debating society, it must have a dependable legal code and courts to interpret it.

Second, the code will be worthless unless there is power somewhere in the background to enforce it.

Third, such power must be vested in a genuine world police force, above and beyond the control of any single state or any probable concert of states.

Fourth, it follows that nations can no longer be sovereign, either in theory or in practice, and the era of nationalism comes to an end. That most vital right of nationalism, the right to arm, to protect oneself, to make war, is abandoned.

This is what the editors of *The New Yorker* meant when they said, "You can't have your anarchical society and eat it too." You can't tell Mexico where she gets off, and have a world state too. You have to accept what the World Legislature, sitting perhaps at Delhi, directs about Mexico. You may have to let other folks determine the fate of the Monroe Doctrine and the Panama Canal. The men of good will have too often overlooked these sharp, painful considerations. They have seen the rose without her thorn.

We cannot be the military big shot in our hemisphere and also accept a superior world police power. We can surrender our freedom of action and take a chance on a warless world via the Parliament of Man. In that Parliament we should be outvoted on a population basis about 18 to 1.

Gentlemen, do you want a world state at that price in 1946? Or do you follow Earl Russell, who said, in the Alabama case after the Civil War: "That is a question of honor which we will never arbitrate, for England's honor can never be made the subject for arbitration." Fortunately England had a two-power navy at the time. Is the Panama Canal subject to arbitration, or is it bound up with the honor of America?

International "Law"

There is no such thing as International Law. What is wrongly called by that name is nothing but international *usage*. If a nation is sufficiently strong, it can add a new usage at any moment. We Britishers have made ourselves guilty of more breaches of international agreements than any other nation. We have often used our sea power in order to make surprise attacks on other countries. . . . It cannot be stressed too often that international law merely protects the strong, and that the only laws recognized by the Great Powers as binding, are those of might and military preparedness.[3]

Major Murray wrote this before the Kaiser and Hitler had performed their treaty-smashing prodigies. In a revised edition he might well have passed the accolade from Britain to Germany. Within the year, Russia has tossed aside her ten-year pact with Poland and has annexed a third of it, with the wry consent of her allies.

When Mr. Justice Jackson said in 1941 that the "present aggressive wars are civil wars against the international community," he was perhaps a good poet but a bad historian. There is no international community in any organized sense. A community by definition implies law and order, with a sheriff to enforce it. Who is going to stop a new Hitler from engulfing Czechoslovakia, or

3. Major Stewart L. Murray, *The Future Peace of the Anglo-Saxons,* London, 1905.

Russia from taking another section of Poland? There is no law, no judge, no sheriff, to halt any nation from doing anything it badly wants to do. There may be a "law" against it, but it cannot be enforced. That is what sovereignty means: every nation in the last analysis is the sole judge of its own conduct. If another nation wants to stop that conduct, it must fight. There is no appeal to anybody or anything but the sword.

How could international law as we have known it settle such issues as these:

Russia demands a warm water port.
Italy demands the neutralization of Suez.
U. S. demands an air base on Trinidad.
Germany demands the return of her colonies.
Spain demands the return of Gibraltar.

Judicial procedure in international law excludes the matter of force and admits only legal right. This is the fundamental reason why serious international political disputes cannot be settled judicially. They can only be settled by war. Would Britain give up Gibraltar because five black-robed gentlemen at The Hague might say she ought to? Would the United States turn over Alaska to an international commission?

A nation that wants to change the status quo has little possibility of doing so unless it fights. Nations that enjoy the status quo are of course morally devastated by such aggressive action. But it is idealistic moonshine to assume that the status quo nations will ever voluntarily surrender their power, move over and let the newcomer expand.

International customs and institutions, such as the Geneva Convention, standard rules for navigation, postal unions, the Red Cross, are of the highest value. But they are purely voluntary; any member state can withdraw from the agreement at any time, as Japan pulled out of the Geneva Convention some years ago. Such agreements should not be confused with the binding force of law *within* a nation.

Balance of Power

"You either have an international police force," says Professor Quincy Wright, "or you have a balance of power. The League of Nations straddled between the two."[4]

The balance of power is one way to keep the peace, lacking a world sheriff. It is not an infallible way. Britain practiced it during her great days in the following fashion: On the Continent, alliances were constantly forming and dissolving between France, Prussia, Austria, the Low Countries, Russia, Spain, Italy. When one country or one alliance looked ominously strong and about to dominate Europe — as Napoleon once did — Britain would throw in her weight with the opposition. She had plenty to throw and thus she *balanced* the situation. The party which aspired to domination thought it over and often kept the cavalry behind the frontier.

It is interesting to remember that after the Boer War Britain was no longer strong enough to enforce this balancing feat. She forsook the role and made hard-and-fast commitments with France and Russia in the Triple Entente.

The historical conditions which enabled Britain to assume the role will hardly come again. There has been no true balance of power apparatus for forty years. What the world has had since, and what we may or may not have after the war, might better be called *power politics,* though not in the disparaging sense. The

4. *Fortune,* "Round Table," March 1941.

alternative to the world state is the power politics of the Great Powers. This would include of course such alliances and agreements as the Great Powers might make, and such leagues and international agencies as they might set up.

The League of Nations

One would speak with less assurance about these matters if the sad history of the League of Nations were not continually before one's eyes. It has been a great, if somber, teacher, one whose lessons a statesman disregards at his peril.

The League has been the major exhibit in international machinery in our time. All nations were supposed to be represented but the United States Senate prohibited Wilson from joining his own creation. The League had, however, no police power beyond economic sanctions, whereby an "aggressor" might have his imports cut off. When the League first organized it was felt that the morals of Germany and Russia made them unsuitable for membership. Thus three of the seven Great Powers were out of it at the start. Britain and France pretty well ran the inner council, and the prime interest, especially of France, was in preserving war gains and maintaining the status quo.

Despite this unfortunate beginning, the League performed a number of useful functions. Several small wars were halted; a bitter argument between Finland and Sweden was composed. Some excellent medical work was done, such as controlling typhus, while the international opium traffic and the white slave traffic were checked. The League's world statistics were the best to be had, and the International Labor Office, a kind of League subsidiary, did yeoman service in helping to standardize working conditions throughout the world.

After the depression set in, however, the League fell into

deeper and deeper difficulty. It was a fair weather sailor. Japan took advantage of Europe's economic collapse to attack Manchuria. Mr. Stimson, then our Secretary of State, offered to proceed against Japan under the Nine-Power Treaty. But the League, in the person of Sir John Simon, refused cooperation. Britain at the time did not want to take a strong line in the Far East.

The next acid test was Ethiopia. Although Italy and Ethiopia were League members, Mussolini announced that he was going to swallow the Lion of Judah. Again the United States government offered to punish Italy by shutting off oil supplies, "only to find," said Hamilton Fish Armstrong, "that Great Britain and France had no intention of making their threats effective."[5] So even economic sanctions failed, and the Lion of Judah was accordingly engulfed.

Next came the war in the Gran Chaco, between Bolivia and Paraguay. An embargo was imposed on Paraguay. The United States — still not a member — adhered to the ruling. But League member nations turned the sanctions into a farce by open smuggling.

The Civil War in Spain broke out. The League did nothing. In 1937, China was wantonly attacked by Japan. The League passed a pious resolution. Finally, Hitler seized Austria and partitioned Czechoslovakia, both League members, in violation of the solemn agreements which the League was supposed to guarantee. It was Neville Chamberlain who at this point declared:

> The League of Nations as constituted today is unable to provide collective security for anybody. . . . We must not try to delude small and weak nations into thinking that they will be protected by the League against aggression . . . when we know that nothing of the kind can be expected.

5. *We or They,* Macmillan, New York, 1938.

It is not difficult to draw three conclusions from this melancholy history:

1. A League which is really going to stop war must include *all* the Great Powers.

2. It must have military as well as economic power, and not be afraid to use either when a member kicks over the traces.

3. It must be ready to *change* the status quo by international law when conditions seem to warrant it. Otherwise the only possible method of change is by violence.

If these conditions are met, the name "League" becomes an anomaly, and the sturdier "Federation," if not World State, should be substituted. In brief, the history of the League of Nations from 1919 to 1939 strongly indicates that only a world state can stop wars and allow for peaceful change by legal means.

Another League

Out of this war an alliance of the victors — Russia, Britain and the United States — seems to be coming. At Dumbarton Oaks in 1944, the outlines for a new League were drafted, and at San Francisco adopted by the United Nations. By no stretch of the imagination should this draft be confused with a world state. Rather it is a mechanism through which the will of the Big Three can operate in a more orderly fashion than through normal diplomatic channels. It will provide a forum where little nations may air their grievances. It can resurrect and carry on the medical and statistical functions of the old League. But it is a variety of power politics, not a federation of the world, as we shall demonstrate more fully in the next chapter.

Why can't we have the latter? Most civilized people want it. A large majority of Americans, according to opinion polls, favor it. It is coming as surely as the sunrise. Where is the hitch? One hitch seems to be that the American government is afraid of it, and that neither the British nor the Russians will have anything to do with it.

Another hitch is the tremendous disparity in culture, race, living standards, education, religious beliefs, ideologies, languages, among the two billion members of homo sapiens in this year of 1945. A world state needs a basic cultural unity to operate. W. F. Ogburn warns of "the essential weakness of a league or association, as compared with the inherent strength of a society or community."[6] *Union Now* was based on cultural similarity, embracing as it did only the democracies. But it left out most of the world. There is no political democracy in Russia, China, India, Japan, the Near East, and not much in Latin America. How much there will be in Europe after the war is anybody's guess. Maybe Dumbarton Oaks is the nucleus for an ultimate unity, but obviously it will need years to grow.

"A world government," says John K. Jessup in *Life*, "is almost certainly not coming out of this war. If something calling itself that is set up, it will be a fraud." No Great Power has yet offered to accept the jurisdiction of a world state, nor is any likely to. I cannot see that this is cause for despair. A citizen would have to be pretty far up in the clouds to believe, after watching the performance of the old League, that a world state was imminent. I have advocated it for twenty years, but I do not expect to live to see it, any more than I seriously expect to see billboards taken off the highways — a reform I have advocated even longer.

What we can hope for is a series of agreements about specific things — relief, reconstruction, an international bank, wheat, cotton, oil, the drug traffic, cartels, Olympic games, an interna-

6. George B. de Huszar, editor, *New Perspectives on Peace,* University of Chicago Press, Chicago, 1944.

tional court, copyrights, fisheries, nutrition, migratory birds, control of epidemics, airways, merchant marines — the list of useful functions is practically endless. Such agreements can help to weave the world together, help to bring our ideologies, folkways, living standards, close enough so that the world state becomes a practical possibility.

Just one thing, in my opinion, could force a genuine world state in the next few years, and that would be such a devastating new weapon as the atomic bomb. If it is as lethal as claimed, the leaders of the Great Powers might no longer dare to trust to their own strength. Then they might be willing to surrender sovereignty.

10

THE BIG THREE

THE UNITED STATES, RUSSIA AND BRITAIN

AT THE SAN FRANCISCO PARLEY in 1945 on the Dumbarton Oaks proposals it was customary and courteous to speak of the Big Five, including France and China. But France and China are not Great Powers at the present time.

The London *Economist* has defined a Great Power as one "capable of waging active and autonomous war against another Great Power.... It must be able to fight with its own resources — not necessarily with those to be found in its own territories, but those that it can rely on being able to procure." Bernard Shaw puts it this way: "The sort of armament that decides modern wars is so enormously expensive, and needs such a big organization of industry, that small states are virtually disarmed at present. . . ."[1]

No nation can fight without modern weapons, and that means great blocks of inanimate energy available, vast mass production capacity, and batteries of research laboratories. There are only five industrial units in the world which can fight a modern war. Two have been defeated and occupied. That leaves three. Here power will reside for the indefinite future.

1. Interview reported in the *New York Herald Tribune*, August 27, 1944.

World Revolution

From one point of view, as we noted in *The Road We Are Traveling*, the war is only an incident in a world revolution, brought about in large part by the productivity of the machine. The mass of mankind is on the march to share in the benefits of an economy of abundance.

In the West, the revolution is primarily economic. In Asia it takes a racial form, with the simple slogan: "Throw the white exploiters out." We are at a point in history when its revolutionary aspects are high-lighted. All of continental Europe, as it is liberated, tilts sharply toward the Left. Socialists, Communists, Partisans, are everywhere in the ascendant. Hitler and Mussolini are gone, their parties destroyed, but the causes which produced them remain. Europe will gravitate to that Great Power which best answers the revolutionary demand for security and employment.

Power Politics

Following San Francisco it is agreed that the Great Powers will reserve for themselves the right to make war. Any alliances or agreements they may initial will be conditioned by this proviso. Any one of the Big Three can be expected to go to war, if, in the opinion of the government then in control, its national interest demands it. Any or all of them can be expected to be highhanded with the neighbors.

At this point, many men of good will throw up their hands and say it is the same old power politics, the same old imperialistic slaughterhouse, and World War III is just around the corner. Let us try to dig a little deeper. What are the motives for another war? Which of the Big Three is likely to be dissatisfied to the pitch of taking up arms against another, and for what reasons?

What Are They Going to Fight About?

Once these questions are asked, our spirits begin to revive a little. With the defeat of Japan the Big Three have a virtual monopoly of military power, and all will have vast natural resources available. They will be suffering from no inferiority complexes.

Russia will have her buffer states, with 100 million people in them, more or less. Britain will have her Empire, her Mediterranean life line, and the hegemony of Africa. The United States will be supreme in the Western Hemisphere, and will face most of the responsibility for organizing the Pacific. All three will have more "living space" than they know what to do with; none will be bothered with those Have-not blues which caused Hitler to consume so many rugs. None has had to drop bombs on another in the course of liberation.

Again, even if there are obvious bones of contention, Russians, Britishers and Americans, in that order, will be fed up with fighting for a long time to come. It will not be politically smart for their leaders to start a war. It might turn into a domestic revolution. Few of the men fighting World War II have enjoyed it much, while the civilian populations of Russia and Britain have endured agonies. If Germany and Japan can be prevented from manufacturing weapons, what governments anywhere are going to be eager for battle?

Russia has been devastated from Minsk to Stalingrad. For a while, half her industrial potential in Europe was knocked out. Her roads and railroads have been torn to ribbons. Her mines are full of water. The great Dnieper dam must be rebuilt. A hundred cities need major reconstruction. President Roosevelt is said to have been staggered by what he saw at Yalta. For many years the major concern of the people of Russia will be the physical reconstruction of their mauled and riddled country.

By the same token, Britain has an enormous task at home. One house in four has been damaged or destroyed. She has a further ominous task abroad. It may take decades before her export-import balance can be brought into solid equilibrium, and her economic health assured.

Will Russia or Britain care to drop these tasks to fight again?

Ideological Bloodshed

Someone asks if we must not fight Russia because we are capitalist and she is communist. To read the Hearst press, that fight is just around the corner. Did the United States ever fight Russia because she was Czarist and we were democratic? Or because she was Greek Orthodox and we were largely Protestant? Can anyone name a war in the last 300 years waged for purely ideological reasons? Alvin Johnson affirms that "no country has ever gone to war on an ideology. Hitler pretended that he was attacking Russia on account of his hatred of Russian ideology. That was a fraud; he was pursuing the old German *Drang nach Osten*."[2]

So if we will not fight on ideological grounds, that leaves as the most plausible war, one between Russia and the United States over real estate or other tangible possessions. But we are the two greatest Have nations on earth, and our material interests clash at no point. We have no common frontier. The nearest we touch on the map is at one of the coldest, bleakest, foggiest, meanest spots on earth.

It is hard to see a direct cause of conflict. What we should guard against is rivalry for influence over *other* nations.

2. *New School Bulletin,* May 1945.

Russia and Europe

A solution for Germany has always been central in the European problem. The Russians are well aware of this, and are concentrating their attention on the German settlement above everything else. If Britain should try to line up Germany against Russia, and solicit our aid again, World War III becomes conceivable. The motive would be the control of all Europe.

Russia is particularly concerned that Germany should not join an anti-Russian bloc with the United States and Britain. This is the only military threat which she really fears. Fritz Sternberg of the New School for Social Research has interpreted her position convincingly. "The Russians will go the limit to prevent any force from coming to power in Germany which would be willing and able to work with an anti-Soviet coalition. They will seek to participate in the control of all sections of Germany."[3]

Russia will liquidate the Junkers and all other big landlords in her zone of influence in Europe, Mr. Sternberg believes. She will encourage a great increase in *peasant* ownership, and will aid planned economies throughout Europe. She will be glad of United States machine tools, but can get along without them if she has to. She will safeguard and encourage the very considerable industries in Czechoslovakia, Silesia, Austria, and eastern Germany. She will not force the Soviet system in these areas, but will guarantee full employment. "So long as Germany remains under Russian influence Russia will be invincible in Europe."

Mr. Sternberg casts a balance sheet of the Great Powers in Europe which is significant. The Russian assets are:

1. The strongest military and industrial state in Europe.
2. No unemployment within her zone of influence.

3. Fritz Sternberg in *Common Sense*, February 1945. Recent moves of Russia in Germany confirm this.

3. Geographic advantage. She is on the spot, day and night. Britain is across the Channel, and we are 3,000 miles away.
4. No sentimental barriers to action.

The Anglo-American assets are:

1. The gratitude of the liberated countries.
2. Very substantial military power — until the United States forces go home.
3. The vast industrial power of the United States in the background.

The liabilities of the Russians are their severe restrictions on many freedoms. The liabilities of the Anglo-Saxon powers are unemployment, insecurity, and the business cycle. Shrinking from the idea of planning for economic stability, the democracies tend to support feudal and reactionary groups in Europe. This is a grave liability not shared by the Russians.

Even if Russia and England agree on dividing and administering Europe, says Mr. Sternberg, England's chickens will turn around and run across the road to Stalin if they are unemployed and miserable. We should recognize "that reactionary policies in Europe and Asia will only aid the further advance of Soviet influence, and that we can only preserve the balance through methods which *in their entirety* are more progressive than those of the Russians." By which Mr. Sternberg means, I take it, that people cannot eat freedom.[4]

The Shape of the Political Structure

We have reached a place in our postwar political speculations where the Big Three dominate the world by their monopoly of fire power. They *could* fall out, but the chances seem to be against

4. The British Labor Party, following its victory over Mr. Churchill, may take a more liberal line in Europe.

it for some years to come. During this period, the world state may begin to look not only alluring, but politically possible. Many things can happen in a long armistice, not all of them unpleasant.

Very good. The Big Three will make, indeed have made, certain agreements about keeping the peace, about getting the wheels of the world turning again. Agreements will not have the validity of law, but they can be useful if people understand they are not law. The Big Three can set up a series of agencies to promote specific international projects, like a world bank, or the operation of planetary airways. Conferences for a number of such agencies have already taken place, as we shall note later.

Finally, the Big Three at Dumbarton Oaks drafted a new League of Nations, which would, among other things, give formal representation to the rest of the world. This, too, can be a useful organization, *if not represented to be more than it is.*

Dumbarton Oaks and San Francisco

If one crosses the Massachusetts Avenue bridge over Rock Creek in Washington, and then takes a pleasant footpath along the stream to the left, he will presently come to a dignified stone entrance under great shade trees, with the inscription "Dumbarton Oaks." In the mansion behind this stone gate discussions went on for many weeks in the hot Washington summer of 1944, and proposals finally were drafted.

In the spring of 1945, delegates from fifty United Nations met at San Francisco to consider these proposals. There was a "crisis" over the chairmanship, a crisis over the admission of Argentina, a crisis over the veto power, and a perpetual crisis over Poland. The press loves a fight and it made the most of the crises, but at the end of eight weeks the Dumbarton Oaks proposals, together with a few amendments — more minor than major — were ratified.[5] Presently the United States Senate approved the Charter by the overwhelming vote of 89 to 2.

At a colorful ceremony in the classic porticos of the Veterans' Building, two hundred official delegates — ambassadors, foreign ministers, plenipotentiaries, Arab princes in flowing burnooses, and the silver-haired host, Mr. Stettinius — signed the Charter. Texts were given in all five of the official languages — English, Russian, Chinese, French and Spanish. The signing lasted eight hours. It was the culmination of President Roosevelt's life's work, the capstone of a structure he had tried to build out of a series of international documents, namely:

The Atlantic Charter	1941
The United Nations Declaration	1942
The Moscow Declaration	1943
The Dumbarton Oaks Proposals	1944
The Yalta Agreements	1945

Mechanics

The Charter provides for a *General Assembly* where each member nation has one vote. The present membership is fifty, but more can be added. The function of the assembly is to provide an international forum where world problems can be discussed, and to elect six member nations to the *Security Council*.

The Council is the real powerhouse of the organization. The so-called Big Five have permanent seats. The six elected from time to time by the assembly complete a governing group of eleven. Their task is to investigate international disputes, try to

5. The Charter will officially come into existence when it has been approved by the United States, Britain, Russia, France, China, and a majority of the "Little Forty-Five."

settle them by peaceful arbitration, and if this is impossible to take economic and military action.

If the situation is grave enough to call for military action, the *Military Staff Committee,* composed of Chiefs of Staff of the Big Five, limbers up the bombers and the tanks. Each of the member nations is to provide a quota of trained soldiers and equipment which the Military Staff Committee can summon.

An *International Court of Justice* of fifteen members is to settle legal issues among the nations.

An *Economic and Social Council* of eighteen members is to study the fundamental causes of war, and make reports and suggestions.

A *Trusteeship Council,* dominated by the Big Five, is to administer dependent areas. Many islands in the Pacific will keep this council busy.

Finally, the organization may absorb existing international agencies, like the I.L.O., or proposed agencies, like the Bretton Woods Fund and Bank.

Veto

The charter provides that if a charge of aggression is lodged against any one of the Big Five, the defendant can veto action against himself by his vote in the Security Council.

Say the United States seizes Lower California — perish the thought! Mexico brings a charge of aggression. The charge is debated in the Security Council, and a vote is taken. Ten votes are in favor of proceeding against the United States, but the U. S. delegate votes no. *So no action is taken.* The United States retains possession of Lower California. Similarly, Russia and Britain may do whatever their consciences direct. So, theoretically, may France and China.

Appraisal

Certain statements can at once be made about the Charter as it stands (September 1945).

It is not a world state.
It parallels the old League of Nations.
The Big Three control it absolutely, through the Security Council mechanism.
It can stop wars between little nations.
It might be helpful in world economic and social problems.

The task of coercing a Great Power is clearly beyond the scope of the Charter. It has a few more teeth than the old League, but not many more. It can solve none of the really tough political problems, such as what is to be done about Germany, Japan, the Balkans, Poland, the Near East, Hong Kong, Manchuria, the Chinese communist government, and so on and on.

Rather, as the London *Economist* points out, it will be the other way round: If the tough problems can be somehow settled independently, *then the Charter will have a chance to function.*[6] If the leaders of the Big Three genuinely desire to work together for peace, the Charter "can be an effective and creative instrument of their common purpose." Power, concludes the *Economist,* will continue to be with the leaders, not with the machinery.

M. Malinin, writing in the Leningrad *Star,* comes to the same conclusion. He says that the Dumbarton Oaks proposals make stimulating reading, but "the independence of small nations after the war will depend on the benevolence of the big nations."[7]

So we are going to have another League of Nations, and try again. Mr. Wilson's League, which the Senate did not permit him

6. September 23, 1944; see also issue of October 14, 1944.
7. Quoted by Louis Fischer in *The Nation,* September 16, 1944.

to join, was dominated by Britain and France. The new one will be dominated by Britain, Russia and the United States. The old failed dismally, as we have seen. Will this one do better? It depends on the Big Three. If they can keep out of each other's hair, machinery is here available which can prove useful: stop little wars, perhaps discourage big ones, knit the world more closely together, allow time for more fundamental steps.

From a broader point of view, no paper constitution or charter can guarantee peace. The causes of war lie far beneath the action of any government, no matter how arbitrary, reckless or violent. Some of the causes lie in trade routes — sure to be greatly disarranged on the new world maps; in supernational businesses or cartels; in raw material markets — sure to emerge from war controls transformed beyond recognition; in mass unemployment and mass migration.

Other causes are still psychological mysteries. What powerful human emotions make up the sentiment we call patriotism — which we solemnly praise as a virtue or condemn as a vice, according to the geographic accident of where one was born? What is the meaning of "fear," "inferiority," "honor," on a national scale? What explains the power of a single man to set a country's war machine in motion? Can people want peace in their conscious minds and at the same time unconsciously desire war? May war not seem preferable to starvation, unemployment or sheer boredom?

Perhaps the Economic and Social Council of the new Charter can find some answers to these questions. Its membership would seem to be of the first importance. What we want is not great names, but modern thinkers, as disinterested as physicists and as humble as astronomers. It is hard for a doctor to cure a disease he does not understand. War is a disease afflicting the whole human race; so considered it may be curable.

In the light of these questions, it is still more dubious how far we can enforce peace on the philosophy of punishing "aggressors." A nation is not a person. Individuals can be guilty of this and that, but a "guilty nation" is a mad concept. To believe in it is to undermine all faith in humanity and the brotherhood of man. If babes in arms, little children, hurt and puzzled housewives, the average citizen who does not want to be shot or thrown into a concentration camp for defying his armed leaders — if such are "guilty," and they comprise at least 95 per cent of the population of any nation, including Germany and Japan, then we are all guilty.

And perhaps, in a way, we are. We the people, have not yet cared enough about stopping wars to do anything effective in that direction. World War I was unpleasant for a lot of people, including civilians, and World War II has proved even more so. The time may come when we the people may really revolt against war. Then we will not need any timid, ten per cent Charters. We can put the best brains on the planet to work, analyzing and organizing for us. Then at last we shall be able to go all out for a genuine world state.

11
NEW ROADS

THE BIG THREE constitute the political core of the postwar world. They will determine the shape of tomorrow's trade.

There appears to be no important group in any nation, except the United States, that demands a return to nineteenth century orthodoxy in foreign commerce. On the other hand, nobody anywhere is celebrating the methods of 1919 to 1939. Is there not a compromise road, which provides for more multilateral action and freer trade than we had before the war, without trying to restore the old gold standard?

Lord Keynes has been at work on this problem for some years. He produced, as you remember, a plan for an international bank in 1943. Not long after, the U. S. Treasury released the so-called White plan with a similar objective. Discussion was world-wide, even the Russians joining in. Finally representatives of the United Nations met at Bretton Woods in New Hampshire in the spring of 1944 to draft a plan on which all countries might agree. After many weeks of deliberation under the shadow of Mt. Washington, proposals for an International Currency Stabilization Fund and an International Reconstruction Bank were duly voted and placed upon the table for acceptance by the governments of the world. In July 1945, Congress accepted them.

Bretton Woods is an attempt "to find a mechanism acceptable to all parties to accomplish the purposes formerly achieved by the gold standard," says Dr. Michael A. Heilperin.[1] Without some control the currency of a nation with a deficit in its international balance tends to depreciate in value, and the depreciation may spread to other countries. The Fund is designed to check such depreciation before it assumes epidemic proportions. The Bank is a long-range plan to make funds available at reasonable rates of interest, for worth-while projects which otherwise could *not* be financed in the regular capital markets.

Bretton Woods, as Dr. Heilperin sums it up, is a compromise between economic nationalism and the need for international collaboration. He thinks no other solution is politically possible at the present time.

It remains to be seen whether even this solution is possible. Certainly it is a new road, never traveled before, and worth trying. The alternative seems to be a continuation of the funny money business of the interbellum period.

No sooner was the ink dry on the proposals at Bretton Woods than important American bankers began to take exception to them. Why? Because they scented managed economies, preferred to go all the way back to 1870, and did not want to compromise. But if Bretton Woods should not be accepted and put into operation, they will get not 1870 but something more like 1938. As Jacob Viner puts it:[2]

The United States is, in effect, as concerns leadership, very nearly single handed, trying to reverse the whole trend of policy and practice of the world at large since 1914, and especially in the ill-fated years

1. *International Monetary Reconstruction*, American Enterprise Association, New York, 1945.
2. *International Financial Stabilization*, Irving Trust Co., New York, 1944.

since 1929. . . . The really important decision will be made by us as to whether we really wish these objectives to be seriously pursued. The question of the most effective ways and means for promoting their realization is only of secondary importance.

Russia, with her state monopoly, has no particular interest in multilateral trading. The British, as we shall see presently, have powerful interests strongly opposed to it. That leaves the United States, as Dr. Viner says, the chief advocate among the Big Three. So if Bretton Woods is thrown out the cause of multilateral trading will be lost indeed.

Let us now look at some of the specific provisions.

The Fund

When the Germans were hurriedly evacuating Paris in the summer of 1944, a Scotsman found himself in town with £2,250 in Bank of England notes. As the master race took to its heels, German officers and soldiers scrambled to convert the marks and francs in their pockets into pounds and dollars. In the scramble, the pound was bid up to 4,000 francs. At this point, the canny Scotsman converted his pounds into 9 million francs. When the Allies took over Paris, the franc was officially pegged at 50 to the dollar. So the Scotsman proceeded to convert his 9 million francs into $180,000. This put him in a position, at the going dollar-pound ratio, to collect £45,000 for the £2,250 he had started with a few days earlier.[3]

This little story makes redundant any further comment on the necessity of stabilizing postwar currencies.

Nations participating in the Fund, according to the plan of Bretton Woods, agree to price their currencies in terms of gold and hence in terms of each other. Rates cannot be altered more

3. *Fortune*, November 1944.

than 10 per cent, except after consultation with the Fund authorities. This would guard against such cataclysmic changes in rates as took place after 1931. To aid stability, the Fund stands ready to make short-term loans to support currencies which are weakening. The loans would come from a pool established by 44 nations. As the strongest nation of all, the United States puts up $2.75 billion in gold and currency. Britain contributes $1.3 billion, Russia $1.2 billion, and so on down the line. The United States gets about 28 per cent of the votes on the control board of the Fund, to correspond with its 28 per cent cash contribution.

Let us take a hypothetical case of the Fund in operation. Guatemala, let us say, is in a jam. She cannot cover her essential imports by exports plus loans. So she applies to the Fund for help. The directors investigate carefully and find that orders are on the books for Guatemala's superb coffee, and she will balance out all right in the end if she has some temporary assistance. The Fund gives her dollars, or pounds, or some other strong currency, out of its pool in exchange for her quetzals. Guatemala uses the dollars to settle her imports, recovers her international balance, and presently redeems her quetzals.

Suppose Guatemala does not regain her economic strength, and pay back? According to the plan, the stabilizing loans which the Fund can make to any one country are *strictly limited*. They depend on the original contribution of that country, of which only 25 per cent can be borrowed in any one year. Thus the risk of net loss is slight. The whole United States contribution of $2.75 billion is the equivalent of running our war machine for ten days. That is no reason why we should throw $2.75 billion away. But it seems a relatively small risk to achieve a large degree of stability.

The reader may ask why this plan is not a return to the international gold standard. True, postwar currencies are to be priced in terms of gold, *but the rates can be changed* after due notice and consultation with the Fund authorities. The rates are managed. The old gold standard was supposed to be unmanaged and automatic; rates were never changed.[4] Even to think of "devaluating," or changing them showed moral turpitude.

Each nation in the Bretton Woods Fund has a "line of credit" approximately equal to its own contribution. Each agrees not to depreciate its currency in competition with other nations, and to refrain from issuing "blocked" currencies, special currencies, and other funny money practices. If, however, a member has "blocked" currency outstanding, as Britain has, it is allowed five years to clean up the situation and get into line.

The Bank

The purpose of the Bretton Woods plan for an International Bank is to finance postwar reconstruction projects that otherwise would not be built. Like the Fund, the Bank has a pool to which more than 40 nations contribute, and from which each may borrow — though there is no explicit "line of credit," as in the Fund. The Bank will be capitalized at $9.1 billion to start with, rising to $10 billion when neutrals come in. If the Bank makes a good record, resources may be enlarged.

The United States contribution at the start is $600 million, but as loans are guaranteed our obligation will rise. We will vote 30 per cent of the stock of the Bank. Only 20 per cent of the Bank's resources may be loaned directly; 80 per cent will be for guaranteeing loans. Clients will usually be governments.

Suppose the Dutch government wants to rebuild its bombed-

4. As we saw in Chapter 4, even the old gold standard began to be managed when the Central Banks made their appearance.

out dyke system, and restore agricultural production. It borrows the money on its own money market in Amsterdam, but the Bank, after investigation, guarantees the loan. This will give a lower interest rate, of course. More dykes can be rebuilt, more sea water pumped out, reconstruction speeded, because of the Bank.

If the Bank floated its own bonds in the securities markets of the world, it would have additional cash to make loans for reconstruction. "The Bank," says *Fortune,*[5] "would thus regularize loans to foreign governments which in the 1920's proved such a pain in the neck to American investors."

Or Else

The Bretton Woods proposals are opposed by certain bankers in the United States, as we noted earlier. Mr. Winthrop W. Aldrich, of the Chase National Bank, complains that "credit extension is not a substitute for sound commercial policies."

The banker's recipe for "sound" commercial policy is as old as the medieval practice of bleeding patients, which in a way it resembles. The *Economist* defines it as "balanced budgets, absence of inflation, funding of floating debts, interest rates unpegged, price and rationing controls removed, and free competition restored. The restoration of a true gold standard — and perhaps of 10,000,000 unemployed — fits admirably into this setting of 'soundness.' "[6]

A powerful school of English bankers and industrialists does not want Bretton Woods either, but for precisely opposite reasons. *They want to protect Britain and the sterling bloc from multilateral trading.* The Fund was really a bargain between Lord Keynes and the U. S. Treasury, whereby Britain agreed to work

5. September 1944.
6. Essay on Mr. Aldrich, September 23, 1944.

toward a multilateral system, while we agreed to allow flexibility in setting exchange rates, and to let Britain use exchange controls for five years.

If the Fund is not accepted, then Britain will be released from her bargain. She can set up a new system of Imperial Preferences and insulate her economy against the United States. The British anti-Bretton Woods school is in deadly fear of two things: Having what they call the "prison bars of the gold standard" forced on them, and being dragged into the vortex of a big postwar depression in the United States. There is a chance that the new British government may reject Bretton Woods on these grounds.

The British sincerely debate whether any universal multilateral, stable currency exchange system is possible or desirable in the postwar world. For Americans there is no debate. Such a system is the only one being supported. We debate whether the system shall take the form of Bretton Woods or the nineteenth century. Says Keith Hutchison after his visit to England:[7]

Many Britons with whom I discussed the question, while agreeing that freely convertible currencies and multilateral international trade represented the ideal, hastened to add that they were not prepared to sacrifice full employment to attain it. Unless, therefore, the United States was willing to join Britain in adopting positive plans to insure full employment, they felt that the disadvantages of Bretton Woods outweighed its advantages, for free exchanges were the swiftest carriers of the germs of depression.

It would seem better, as the National Planning Association points out, for U. S. citizens to present a united front. If we back out, multilateral trading is doomed. All nations will continue their bilateral deals. "Private interests in the United States would then have to face the necessity of competing, or bargain-

7. *The Nation*, March 3, 1945.

ing with, powerful state-controlled economic units. Bilateral agreements and manifold discriminations would become the rule. . . ."[8]

Internationalism a la Carte

Bretton Woods is only one exhibit in a whole museum of actual or possible international agencies which can draw the nations closer together in cooperative endeavors and so strengthen the nucleus of a world state.

The International Labor Office has been improving labor standards throughout the world for many years. It is now battling for an agreement between governments to maintain full employment in domestic economies.

UNRRA is acting as a good Samaritan with forty-four nations contributing to its chest.

At White Sulphur Springs in 1943, delegates from the United Nations prepared strong recommendations for the food supply of the planet. Congress has supported them.

At Chicago in 1944, other delegates debated — with the conspicuous absence of Russia — planetary airways.

Conferences have been called, or are on the agenda, for oil, cotton, wheat, rubber, copper, shipping.

Conferences will also be needed for problems of migration and resettlement; for encouraging international commercial arbitration; for widening access to essential raw materials; for coordinating employment; for the atomic bomb.

Commodity Agreements

Sovereign states may not be able to agree about the principles of war and peace, but they can agree, and have agreed, about

8. "The Stakes of Bretton Woods," National Planning Association, Washington, April 1945.

sugar, sock-eyed salmon, and many other specific commodities. This all helps international good will, especially if nations which consume the commodities, as well as those which produce them, are represented on the control boards.[9]

At the turn of the century a dozen nations were dumping sugar on the world market, depressing the price and ruining farmers. The Brussels Sugar Convention of 1902 ended the dumping by a series of agreements whereby each country exporting sugar was given a quota on the world market. Prices rose; beet and cane growers had some relief. Other agreements have restricted competitive fishing and promoted the conservation of halibut, salmon, fur-bearing seals, and whales.

Although these agreements between governments about specific commodities can be called "cartels," it is difficult to find much harm in them. True, they restrict free competition, but also they conserve resources which otherwise might be destroyed by unlimited competition, and save whole categories of farmers from bankruptcy. Sometimes, as in the case of opium, or a surplus of sugar, trade needs restraining. After the war, surplus trouble will probably appear in the following products:

Rubber	Sugar
Cotton	Coffee
Silk	Copper
Wheat	Machine tools
Fats and oils	Aluminum
Ships	Magnesium

One way to get rid of the surplus is to dump it abroad at prices below home costs, another is to dump it into the ocean, an-

9. See I.L.O., *Intergovernmental Commodity Control Agreements*, Montreal, 1943. Here are the texts of all important agreements, with introductory remarks. A gold mine of information.

other is to force it on the natives by high pressure imperialism. These ways have all been tried and left a good deal to be desired. Perhaps a better way is to have a "Bretton Woods" plan for critical commodities, as well as for currencies and credit.

Cartels

Back in the days when Thurman Arnold was teaching law at Yale, one didn't have to go behind the barn to say the word "cartel" out loud. It was quite a respectable word then, especially in the sense of commodity agreements. Today, thanks in part to Judge Arnold, "cartel" has become a very naughty word indeed, and it is therefore difficult to discuss the subject rationally. Here we only have the space to make a few brief comments:

"Cartel" is a label usually referring to an arrangement between firms in two or more countries to avoid, or modify, competition. When the government becomes a party to the arrangement, it may or may not be called a commodity agreement. In 1939, the Department of Justice listed 179 cartel agreements, of which 109 included American enterprises.[10] Eight of the 179 had to do with crops; thirty-two with minerals; six with services like shipping, the rest with manufactured goods, like optical instruments and chemical products. In 1938, according to one estimate, cartels controlled about one third of all international trade.

The agreements normally fell into four classes according to their purpose: (1) to fix prices; (2) to restrict production among members; (3) to divide world markets among members; (4) to cross-license patents and research discoveries.

The motives for forming a cartel are mixed. It is not without significance that more cartels were formed after the 1929 smash than at any other period in history. Apparently the motive was to

10. Corwin Edwards, *American Economic Review,* January 1944.

avoid loss, rather than to scalp the consumer. "The beginnings of depressions," says Corwin Edwards, "abound in efforts to organize cartels." We see operating here the same motive which was powerful in forming domestic monopolies in the 1870's — the desire of businessmen to shelter themselves from the raging storms of the free market.[11]

Plenty of cartels and monopolies, however, have been motivated by no reason but unadulterated greed. The files of the Department of Justice are full of evidence on this point.

Obviously the United States cannot eliminate cartels, no matter how bad they may be, if Britain and Russia want to continue them. We can stop their doing business in the United States, and perhaps stop United States firms from participating in them abroad, but if two members of the Big Three do not cooperate in our campaign, what can we do about that?

If we go it alone, we may make it impossible for Americans to do business abroad. "In many countries," says Ralph W. Gallagher, of Standard Oil of New Jersey, "free competition does not exist. In its stead we find control of production, markets and prices."[12] To go into Iraq at all, Standard had to become a party to restrictive agreements with British, Dutch and French oil interests. Maybe Standard had no business in Iraq, but there it is.

The best solution, in my opinion, would be another international agency, like Bretton Woods, sponsored and enforced by the Big Three. We might call it the International Cartel Authority. It could go right to work and prevent German cartels from reorganizing. It might then proceed to a system of licensing all

11. See *Democracy Under Pressure,* Chapter 6, "Are Monopolies Inevitable?" Twentieth Century Fund, New York, 1945.
12. Statement before the O'Mahoney Committee of the Senate, May 1944.

international cartels, or at least making public their provisions — the goldfish bowl technique.

A cartel by definition is on a supragovernmental level, above all existing governments. Thus it is responsible to nobody. It is one dynamic example that shows how national political structures fail to agree with economic and technical realities. A world state could hold cartels to account as modern governments hold domestic business; and an international agency that could meet this need successfully might do more to unify the world than all the cultural projects ever attempted.

12

ON THE HOME FRONT

Before drafting a home-front program, we might do well to tack up on the wall in plain sight a list of the paradoxes which often beset American programs for foreign commerce. "Our pronouncements," says Robert Chandler, "and our practice simply do not hang together."[1]

1. Our leaders almost to a man assure the rest of us that trade must be freed from barriers and restrictions. Whereupon Congress gives another salvo of subsidies to export crops.

2. American businessmen are as one in advocating free private trade, but powerful groups among them support the highest tariff walls in history.

3. Some of us denounce government purchasing monopolies, but others scramble to get Russian business after the war — which clears through a government monopoly.

4. We do not believe in dumping goods abroad at fire-sale prices, but we practice it.

5. We denounce cartels, but Americans participated in more than a hundred of them before the war, and many big firms propose to go right on.

6. We decry government interference in business, yet some of us go running to the government whenever things get hot. For instance, when the British government helps British businessmen in the Middle East, we clamor for our government to help American businessmen.

1. *The Nation*, July 28, 1945.

7. We think exports are wonderful, but many of us will fight bitterly to keep out imports to balance them.

8. We demand stiff reparations from Germany, but refuse to take German goods — which is the only way reparations can be paid.

9. Many of us are still enchanted with a "favorable balance of trade," which actually makes the nation poorer in physical goods.

Full Employment the Major Remedy

I asked Sir Henry Bunbury, chairman of the British planners, the P.E.P., what he thought we should do about our tariff to further international cooperation. He replied: "Do anything you like about it. Have it high or medium or low. Have free trade or autarchy, it makes little difference — provided you do one thing."

"And that?"

"Provided you keep out of a depression!"

John Maynard Keynes argues along the same line when he says:[2]

. . . If nations can learn to provide themselves with full employment by their domestic policy . . . there need be no important economic forces calculated to set the interest of one country against that of its neighbors. . . . International trade would cease to be what it is, namely, a desperate expedient to maintain employment at home by forcing sales on foreign markets and restricting purchases, which, if successful, will merely shift the problem of unemployment to the neighbor which is worsted in the struggle — and would become a willing and unimpeded exchange of goods and services in conditions of mutual advantage.

When every nation tries to relieve unemployment at home by forcing goods abroad, often at fire-sale prices, the world comes to the impasse it reached in the thirties. The preposterous condi-

2. Quoted by C. E. Ayres in *The Emancipator*, Summer, 1942.

tion arises of a market composed of eager sellers and sullen buyers. Trade becomes a one-way street — at least the emphasis is
all in one direction. The result is a wholesale exporting of unemployment from country to country. Instead of vainly trying
to create employment by forcing exports abroad, we should plan
for home employment by other means and then enjoy the gain in
both exports and imports which is likely to follow.

How should we plan? Lord Keynes advocates a compensatory
economy where fiscal policy, taxation, social security, public
works, and encouragement to venture capital are all used to
check booms and slumps, and steady the trade cycle.[3]

Full employment requires three policies, all of which are
within the domestic control of a large country:[4] *First,* to spend
enough — consumers, business and government. *Second,* to plan
training and work enough, so as to match workers and jobs.
Third, to manage the location of industry enough to keep workers from constantly moving their homes.

Understanding these policies, says Mr. Coyle, "frees the British, or any industrial country, of the supposed necessity of dumping its goods abroad merely to keep its workers occupied. . . .
Foreign trade thus becomes not a way of making jobs but a way
of obtaining materials with which to raise the standard of living.
. . . If the great powers can cease to regard trade as a vehicle for
dumping their unemployment on less powerful nations, if they
can buy and sell purely for the sake of obtaining what they need
and paying for it, the prospects of a harmonious world will be
bright. Americans so far have shown only faint glimmerings of
this principle." Mr. Coyle believes that the British have mastered

3. See the compensatory plan in book 3 of this series, *Where's the Money
Coming From?;* also the Murray Full Employment Bill.
4. Following David Cushman Coyle in the *Survey Graphic,* May 1945.

the principle. As assistant to Ambassador Winant, he has a good listening post.

The *Economist* calls full employment the cornerstone of foreign commerce. Beardsley Ruml and E. C. Sonne hold that high employment, with corresponding high imports, is "perhaps the greatest contribution we can make toward the improvement of world conditions." The British, as we noted in the last chapter, will be more likely to adopt the Bretton Woods proposals if they feel we are going to avoid a postwar depression. Dr. Calvin B. Hoover of the Committee for Economic Development says:

Our volume of imports and exports is itself more affected by changes in depression and prosperity in the United States than it is apparently affected by changes in our tariffs. Putting the matter crudely, if we ask what would increase our exports and imports more than anything else, we would have to answer: Anything that would insure a high level of employment in the United States.[5]

The Bureau of Foreign and Domestic Commerce supports Dr. Hoover with many figures. "The volume of imports," it says, "is affected by many factors . . . but the basic influence is clearly the level of business activity in the United States. The value of imports is high in times of domestic prosperity and low in times of domestic recession. . . . Another way of expressing this relationship is that in the experience of recent years, each increase (or decrease) of $10 billion in the gross national product has been associated with an increase (or decrease) of $500 million in imports."[6] The physical volume of imports follows industrial production. It must, because more than 70 per cent of all imports, by value, have consisted of raw materials for industry.

5. Address at New York University, January 19, 1944.
6. Maffry and Lary, *op. cit.*

Tariffs

The average American associates foreign trade with the protective tariff, and, up to a few years ago, was prepared to get shouting mad about it. No high school graduation used to be complete without a debate on protection vs. free trade. Now it appears that full employment is more important for foreign commerce than reductions in the tariff.

It does not follow that the tariff system is unimportant. Far from it. Many rates are fantastically high. Some have been most useful in building up new industries, in diversifying occupations, in giving the country stand-by capacity in case of war. One cannot generalize safely. The "tariff" is only a meaningless verbal noise until one gets down to cases, asking what schedule is being referred to, for what industry, when?

Mr. Ruml, with his active imagination, sees the United States tariff on shoes, for instance, as a kind of sales tax paid by the U. S. consumer to the U. S. shoe industry.[7] As things are now, the industry is required to make no accounting for this favor. Maybe the "tax" is a wise one, maybe not. We ought to know the final effect of the tax. Mr. Ruml therefore suggests that the protective tariff be abandoned in favor of a *direct subsidy* by the government to those industries that genuinely need fostering in the public interest. This would bring the business out into the open with a bang! Each industry would have to prove it deserved its subsidy. Many, one suspects, would not qualify.

It would be a mistake to believe that American industry is as pious about free enterprise and free trade as it sounds right now (July 1945). Behind the amiable front, the high-tariff forces are drilling their panzer divisions. Many big manufacturers know

7. *Tomorrow's Business,* Farrar and Rinehart, New York, 1945.

that they can meet foreign competition, no matter how low the wage scales of the "pauper labor of Europe," because they rely more on machines than on men to keep their costs at rock bottom. But a whole new crop of industries is lining up for more tariff protection, including lumbermen, miners, silver producers, beef growers, wool growers. The nonferrous metals people are savagely assailing the idea of stock-piling for future emergencies unless *they* provide the material for the piles at several times the cost of importing.

The United States, says Roscoe Fleming, is full of horse-radish growers, and Washington is filled with their sympathetic Congressmen.[8] All are eager for lasting peace and international co-operation. "They are also eager for a protected market for their own particular brands of horse-radish. And they can't have both." There is no doubt that bigger and better tariffs after the war would encourage trade barriers in other countries, and so offset to a degree the beneficent effects of both full employment and Bretton Woods. Worse, if the United States tries to get full employment by forcing exports rather than by building up home purchasing power, and the high tariff bloc shuts off imports, we will incite a savage trade war with Britain. This would be a tragedy, for Britain, as we have seen, has no alternative. She *must* export or die.[9]

The more moderate we can keep our tariffs the better. It is no longer a case of protecting infant industries against the "pauper labor" of this ally or that. It is a case of planning tariff schedules to promote the maximum of world employment and prosperity.

8. "Horse-radish and World Peace," *Harper's*, May 1945.
9. See Smith and Kouwenhoven, "That Export Boom May Cost U S Another War," *Harper's*, February 1945.

Imports First

In so far as nations deliberately plan their foreign commerce it is well to think of imports first. E. H. Carr puts it like this:

> The way to a revival of international trade is not to decide what you want to sell abroad and then ascertain what you are compelled to buy from the foreigner in order to induce him to take it, but to decide what you want to buy from abroad and then ascertain what you must produce in order to pay for it. . . . In preparing for war we do this, which explains why rearmament is good for international trade as well as for trade at home. To bring about the same results in time of peace, we must have the same concentration on the needs of the consumer, and make production, internationally as well as nationally, serve the purposes of consumption.[10]

In 1940, our chief imports by value were rubber, vegetable oils, sugar, coffee, paper and pulp, cloth and clothing, silk, tin, jute and burlap, fruits, hides, furs, raw wool, manganese, nickel. After the war the pattern will change, but we can be sure that our factories and our stomachs will need considerable amounts of imported raw materials. In addition, the government may want to stock-pile some resources, in case of trouble, and help conserve domestic deposits of others — especially petroleum, iron ore, copper, lead and zinc — all minerals which are running short.

My guess, for what it is worth, is that the country will need two to four billion dollars' worth of such essential imports, at 1940 prices, for some years after the war. Whatever agency is charged with protecting our supplies of strategic raw materials, as they should have been protected before Pearl Harbor, must make sure that essential imports are available and in no danger of being cut off. If this violates the 100 per cent free market, it does not violate common sense.

10. *Conditions of Peace.*

Turismo

Over and above an unfailing supply of essential imports would come the desirable imports. Here the free market would be paramount. From one viewpoint, anything for which citizens want to throw their dollars around will be desirable. Let people order what pleases them, short of opium and cobras.

At the same time, plans should be laid for expanding useful imports or their equivalent. How about inviting Americans to fly around the world for $489.75? This would send dollars abroad to balance exports. How about high school youngsters spending their senior year, or part of it, in a surplus Victory merchant ship, inspecting Athens, Hong Kong and Valparaiso, with classes in the main salon every evening? How about a Detroit factory worker of Swedish descent taking his two weeks' vacation in Stockholm, carried by a stratosphere liner?

In 1929 our bill for foreign travel was $700 million. If we have full employment after the war, the total will reach $1.5 billion, more or less automatically, on a doubled national income. Milo Perkins thinks it can be pushed to $2 billion with intelligent planning.[11]

Senator Owen Brewster of Maine has proposed a special tax exemption for businessmen who help their workers to take vacations in foreign lands. He wants to see a million innocents abroad annually. Observe the stuff for stuff balance involved. The government subsidizes citizens to enjoy more foreign travel. Thus foreigners get the dollars they need, and Americans get the benefits of the taxpayers' generosity. Under the old formula, as we saw in detail earlier, foreigners got all the benefits when loans were defaulted.

11. See his article in *The Atlantic Monthly*, September 1945, for the best discussion of *turismo* yet published.

What Else to Balance?

Another proposal to offset exports is the acquisition of military bases in settlement of dollar loans. Bermuda has been mentioned, but with few cheers from the British. Still another proposal is direct investment in American-owned factories abroad. This was a large item before the war, and might be again. Before relying on it too heavily, however, it would be a good idea to ask Messrs. Ford and General Electric how many of their plants have been bombed out. You may find a certain lack of enthusiasm for any more direct investments in Europe. And what is Russia going to do to private property there?

Can the reader think of anything else which really runs into money? If he can, he should be decorated. I have been looking into every closet and behind all the bushes for a long time, trying to find some useful stuff to balance the jolly prophecies of $10 billion of exports a year, and I cannot come within a mile of it.[12] Among the best suggestions are these:

A natural increase in imports, above 1940, due to full employment
— assuming we get full employment.
Military stock piles, if needed.
Conservation measures for petroleum, iron ore, etc.
Increased tourist traffic.
Military bases in exchange for exports.
Direct investments in United States plants abroad.
And, of course, if Congress sees it that way, a decrease in some tariff
schedules.

12. Dean Acheson, speaking to the N.A.M., is reported to have said that we must find markets abroad in the neighborhood of $10 billion, and thus provide 3,000,000 jobs in industry and 1,000,000 in agriculture. The United States Lines are now running a series of advertisements saying that "5,000,000 Americans will depend on foreign trade for their postwar living" — meaning more than $10 billion of exports. The National Planning Association estimates $10.6 billion. (See table page 94.)

In so far as the above do not offset exports shipped out, we shall have to take loans. As repeatedly noted, defaulted foreign loans have given the taxpayers and private investors two master headaches in the last twenty-five years. Let us hope that the Bretton Woods Bank can step into the picture this time and save a third planetary headache.

The Bank should deny all international loans where stuff will not come back for stuff. But the research staff will be aware of Colin Clark's thesis cited in Chapter 4. Professor Clark proves that loans for industrializing a "backward nation" — meaning an agricultural one — have often paid out handsomely in the past, and may again. The United States was once a "backward nation."

Some private or U. S. government loans may be in order to finance the sale of our machine tools, turbines, trucks and other capital goods. The war has greatly expanded our capacity to produce these goods, and it is doubtful if we can use half the output at home. But in making loans it is important to check wage levels and working conditions in the borrower's country. "Only those nations," says Milo Perkins in the article referred to above, "which are making internal progress in educating their people and raising their standards of living, are good credit risks for the long pull."

Summary of Postwar Facts About Foreign Commerce

1. Russia, Britain and America, the Big Three, will constitute the political core of the world. What international projects any one of them does not like will not be undertaken, except in a pretty small way.

2. Some groups in the United States are strong for multilateral trading. Elsewhere in the world the demand is light.

3. The United States, however, in making its case for freer trade, is morally handicapped by having the highest tariff on earth.

4. Bretton Woods or not, Russia will continue to operate her exports and imports as a state monopoly.

5. The British government will dominate exports and imports, and, in the event that Bretton Woods is discarded, has a sterling bloc in readiness. Many Britons prefer the latter.

6. All other nations must follow the leadership of the Big Three. Whether they will naturally fall into a sterling bloc, a dollar bloc and a ruble bloc, remains to be seen.

7. New synthetics, new mineral deposits, new crops in new places, new trade routes, new factories in Brazil, India, Canada and elsewhere, will greatly change the pattern of the flow of goods after the war. The total, however, may not diminish. If the world is prosperous, the total may increase over 1938.

8. There will be surplus trouble in some commodities, such as natural rubber and silk. Our huge inventories of war supplies will also complicate trade.

9. There will certainly be many commodity agreements among governments. There will also be some active cartels, despite their low moral standing in the United States.

10. Germany and Japan will be out of world markets, perhaps for a long time. This will be so much pie for the producers of the Big Three and their friends. It is hard to remember when Germany was not a keen and energetic competitor. Since the Potsdam declaration she is flat on her back.

11. People in Congress, or out of it, who demand that Germany and Japan pay cash reparations should be examined by a competent psychiatrist.

Summary of Program for Better Foreign Commerce

The *first* thing is to apply the compensatory device to maintain full employment at home. The total of private and government outlays must be enough to buy back the total product, with employment at high levels.

The *second* thing is to figure out what we need and want from abroad and arrange to get it in without having it scale high tariff walls.

The *third* thing is to use exports to balance imports on a stuff for stuff basis, and to build up the economic strength and the standard of living of friendly nations.

The *fourth* thing is to adopt the Bretton Woods proposals for better currency and banking, and also other international agencies as they are needed for such things as the control of cartels, air traffic, food, migration and settlement, shipping, oil, wheat, and so on.

The *final* thing, in the words of David Cushman Coyle, is "to throw whatever cold water is handy on the efforts of either government or business to push American goods and services abroad without providing for corresponding imports." Let us have no permanent Santa Claus program.

In Conclusion

Foreign commerce is a difficult subject to deal with because so many Americans make two cardinal assumptions: *first,* that the more trade the better, and *second,* that the freer it is the better. In a general way I have adopted these assumptions throughout this book, but I sometimes wonder.

Suppose these assumptions are untrue? Suppose it will be better for more people if trade is more carefully planned and controlled than before the war? Suppose just getting things on a boat is not such a triumph for humanity after all? I do not pretend to know the answer. Only history will settle that. I do know that the American attitude is not much shared in other countries, and that the world trend since 1914 is to give exports and imports a kind of public utility status.

The United States may be the only place left on earth where a dominant business culture survives after the war. If so, it can hardly go beyond the three-mile limit. We cannot force the Russians and the British to forswear commodity agreements and state cartels. It might be difficult to coerce the Canadians and Mexicans to be more free. We cannot export the Sherman Anti-Trust Act to other nations.

The solution with which history will present us in due course may be worse than the free market of the nineteenth century — though it is difficult to see how it could be worse than the 1930's.

It might be better.

THE TECHNOLOGICAL IMPERATIVE

STANDING HERE in the twilight of the second world war, two diverging roads are discernible into the future. One leads to security and peace. One leads to terror and death. Both are the products of technology. During the war, production has been stimulated to heights beyond all previous imaginings, while weapons have been put into action which may someday make the planet uninhabitable.

Which road shall we take? Perhaps we shall flounder between them, never quite achieving that material abundance which technology promises; never quite destroying ourselves. But the limits, on each side, are clearly visible. At the cost of some oversimplification, let us examine them. The effects on trade between the nations in either case will be great.

THE BRIGHT SIDE

Atomic Bricks

Natural resources always carry a date. They are not wealth for all time, but only in terms of prevailing technology. The Indians in North America, before the white man, had no use for iron ore, bauxite, oil, tungsten, because they had no techniques for working them. Helium was not a natural resource until about 1925, when a method was developed for using the gas in balloons.

Until recently such "waste" materials as sawdust and corn shucks were not considered a valuable resource, and neither was sea water or air. With the development of synthetics and plastics, however, a technical revolution has taken place. Any substance whose molecular structure can be broken down into its constituent atoms, without requiring prohibitive amounts of energy, becomes a valuable natural resource. The atoms can be considered as elemental bricks from which the modern chemist builds up new structures, some of them unknown to nature, some of them of the greatest use to man, some of them cheaper than anything ever known before. We have even learned to dissolve the atomic bricks themselves, and may soon put their fabulous energy to useful work.

The implications of this trend are clear. At some point in the development of the chemistry of synthetics, a country hitherto poor will find itself rich. Those Have-not blues will fade, and with them the martial spirit. Or if the spirit remains, it will not arise from economic causes.

Our present search for substitutes . . . is a search that will not end with the war, and will ultimately make it unnecessary for us to clothe ourselves in the hair and furs of animals, or the fibres grown by plants, or to build with wood and stone. . . . We think chiefly of new ideologies; but the chemists and engineers, who are not thinking of "fascism," "democracy," "communism," but of clothing and feeding mankind in new ways, of building houses of materials that nature never thought of making, are the fomenters of revolution too. Scientists in the past have busied themselves chiefly with harnessing energy; now they are changing matter.[1]

1. W. Kaempffert, science editor, in *The New York Times*, November 23, 1941.

Recently I inspected a beautiful pair of skis made from sea-water. They were a magnesium alloy, and magnesium, as you know, is a constituent of sea salt, now chiefly reclaimed from the ocean.

Plastics

Here is a family of plastics called the "vinyl esters." They are used for women's shoes, for golf jackets, aprons, smocks, capes, rubbers, heel pads, sleeve protectors, shower-bath caps, key chains, cosmetic bags. They can be made hard as an oak plank or pliable as a sponge. Wipe a pair of vinyl shoes with a damp cloth and they are bright and clean again. Coal and limestone are the basic materials. Meanwhile, coal, water and air are broken down and reassembled into nylon for stockings, parachutes and tennis racket strings.

Theoretically a plastic material is one which can be formed to the desired shape by heat and pressure. Many natural resources are poorly adapted to modern assembly-line methods. Every piece of wood is different in grain or texture. No two bales of cotton or sacks of wool are quite the same. But if we go back to atoms and combine *them,* we can make a substance whose characteristics are unvarying. The manufacturer can count on its absolute uniformity as raw material. The effect on the cost of the finished product needs no underlining. Uniformity of material is vital in the interchangeable parts that flow along the conveyor belts for airplanes, automobiles, vacuum cleaners, all sorts of things.[2]

Natural materials must still be shaped by essentially handicraft methods. Wood must usually be whittled, stone chipped, metals pounded. Our most ingenious machines are doing the whittling,

2. Following Jack Schuyler, "The Age of Plastics," *Common Sense*, January 1943.

chipping and pounding. But these operations are discontinuous, and not well adapted to a high-speed, continuous manufacturing process. Plastics are far better adapted, for they have been molded to specification and do not need any whittling, chipping or pounding. "Compare," says Jack Schuyler, "the patient cutting, boring and polishing of grandmother's amber beads with the almost instantaneous molding of plastic ones for daughter's costume jewelry."

Self-Sufficiency

We are not discussing the hot-and-cold-folding-door marvels of the advertising copywriters, which are to leave the consumer gasping when the war is over. The consumer, I suspect, is going to be somewhat disappointed in this department. We are discussing a *revolution in the technique of fabricating materials*, which may not reach its full development for many years. Furthermore, unless a community has access to cheap power in large quantities, it cannot make low-cost synthetics. Here is where Uranium 235 may come in. Granting the power, however, and granting the control of high monopolistic prices, "mankind," says Mr. Schuyler, "has vastly increased the range of possible free choice. Not far ahead lies a world where living standards will no longer depend on favored geographical areas."

Garet Garrett looks in the same direction.[3] He sees technology shaping the world into regions of balanced economy, self-contained in respect to necessities. Conflicts will grow fewer. Civilization will become richer in variety. The distinction between industrial and agricultural peoples will largely disappear. Land will revert to its former balanced ecology as crop growing on its pres-

3. *A Time Is Born*, Pantheon Books, New York, 1944.

ent scale declines. Wasting resources like petroleum and copper will no longer be a problem, for they will have been superseded by materials based on the atoms in growing plants and trees, which, if intelligently cultivated, can yield forever.

Lancelot Hogben develops a similar idea. During the nineteenth century, he says, science promoted greater economic interdependence by virtue of the steamship, the transcontinental railroad, the cable.[4] Free traders made a dogma out of this, shut their eyes and failed to wake when modern chemistry came along. Some branches of science are indeed weaving the world ever closer, but others are bound to foster self-sufficiency. Professor Hogben cites saltpeter from home air as well as by boat from Chile; radioactive sodium from local salts; aluminum soon to be manufactured everywhere from common clays; animal feed from the disintegration of wood pulp; sugar from vegetable waste matter. Nor should we forget that literary chemist who, just for the hell of it, made a silk purse from a sow's ear.

Probably the most important synthetic now in mass production is a substance we call rubber. Natural rubber has never been duplicated in the laboratory and probably never will be. Chemical engineers prefer to call the synthetic rubbers "elastomers." Engineers can build special properties and characteristics to order in elastomers because their molecules are tailor-made. The fundamental building bricks for synthetic rubber are butadiene, acetylene, ethylene, styrene. It can be made from petroleum, or from alcohol, which in turn can be distilled from almost any growing thing — wood, potatoes, corn. If the United States ever retreats to natural rubber, except for a minor mixing agent in certain products, it will mean that our chemical industry has entered its dotage.

4. *Science for the Citizen,* W. W. Norton, New York, 1938.

The Changing Import Pattern

After the war, rubber and silk may be stricken from the list of major essential imports. A decade ago the whole automotive industry would have ground to a standstill without natural rubber. Now we need perhaps only a tenth of what we did — 60,000 tons a year instead of 600,000.

The technological imperative is destined to affect other strategic imports in a similar way. Today we must have them; tomorrow we find a better, cheaper product at home. What will this do to foreign trade? The snap conclusion is that trade will sharply decline. There is no doubt about it in the case of materials which technology has rendered obsolete. Foreign trade in animal products, crops, metals, is bound to shrink.

But trade in manufactured goods, in services, may more than make up for the shrinkage. If world prosperity is maintained, the chances are, as we noted earlier, that the gross volume of international commerce will also be maintained, though the pattern will be very different from 1938. It will include less of the essential stuff which keeps body and soul together, but more of the comforts and luxuries which people like and want.

THE DARK SIDE

Technology is amoral and impersonal. While it abolishes poverty with one hand, it launches atomic bombs with the other. Which hand is the stronger? Since 1914, the destructive one has clearly been the stronger. We crystal-gazers cannot overlook the possibility of mankind blowing itself to pieces with a further development of V-weapons and Uranium 235.

Wiseacres will laugh off gloomy prophecies of this nature. They may be right, but it is sobering to remember what Sir

William Henry White, chief constructor for the British navy, said when he heard of Orville Wright's flight over a battleship in 1909: "The nations of the earth are not disturbed over the likelihood of the aeroplane's possible use in war." Only thirty-five years later, in 1944, a six-ton block-buster from a British bomber sunk the Von Tirpitz, perhaps the most powerful battle-ship afloat.

In World War I, an infantry division went into action with 4,400 horses and 153 motor vehicles, the equivalent of 3,300 mechanical horsepower. In World War II, an armored division has 3,500 motor vehicles of 160 different types, with 400,000 mechanical horsepower! From war to war, the energy of a division has increased more than 120 times!

Major Alexander Seversky points out that Pearl Harbor was not a crushing blow to us because the Japanese struck at our fleet in being, rather than at our industry.[5] With industry intact we could produce other fleets — and promptly did so. But now, he says, "aircraft are growing into mighty battleships of the skies, and a country threatened can no longer stave off disaster while its industry goes into high gear. It must have enough aircraft for immediate and decisive operations, with a single paralyzing knockout blow as the goal envisioned." The enemy will envision the same goal. The fate of us plain people in both countries as the visions are fulfilled is not pleasant to contemplate.

A shadow hung over the deliberations at Dumbarton Oaks and San Francisco. It was the new V-weapon and others worse to come. These inventions point to a kind of warfare which will upset the strategy and tactics of war as we know it today. It may be that even a defeated nation can spring a secret weapon on an

5. *The New York Times,* July 24, 1944.

astonished world, though its industrial plant is under careful inspection all the time. It may be that death will fall from the skies with no preliminary warning whatsoever.

When the attempt at precision bombing eventually gave place to area bombing . . . air warfare definitely assumed the character of an attack on the foundations of civilized life. . . . The flying bomb may tear away the veil of illusion that has so long obscured the reality of the change in warfare — from a fight to a process of destruction. . . . Mechanized warfare still left room for human qualities to play an important part in the fight. Automatic warfare cancels them out. It reduces fighting men and civilians alike to the status of rabbits. . . . The most virile nation would not be able to withstand another, inferior in all natural qualities, if the latter had some superior technical appliance, and were willing to use it, no matter how ruthlessly.[6]

The Anglo-American bombing of German cities fully supports Captain Liddell Hart. It has been called the greatest act of mass-expropriation since the Russian revolution.[7] It completed the work of inflation by wiping out urban real estate, the last remaining asset of the middle classes. An attack on the foundations of civilized life indeed!

Historic Dates

On June 15, 1944, the B-29 Superfortress first went into action over Tokyo, and on June 16 it was announced that V-1, the robot bomb, had descended on England. These two consecutive days will leave a large red mark on the calendar of history. V-2 came less than three months later. President Truman announced the atomic bomb on August 6, 1945, to leave an even bloodier mark on the calendar.

6. B. H. Liddell Hart in *Yale Review*, Spring 1945.
7. See Alexander Böker in *Human Events*, June 6, 1945.

We are assured that the primitive robot models of today will soon be replaced by mechanical monstrosities which will leave the ground impelled by rocket motors, will fly through the lower atmosphere by jet propulsion, and will switch back to rockets when they hit the stratosphere. Air Marshal William A. Bishop — who ought to know — says they will cross the Atlantic in three hours, perhaps less. They will be cheap, easy to make and accurate.[8] Why cannot a flying robot also carry an atomic bomb in its warhead? "The Air Age faces mankind with a sharp choice — the choice between Winged Peace or Winged Death." The Air Marshal has come to regard the world's atmosphere as nothing less than world property, "solely because I can think of no other way in which we can make use of the air globally without courting disaster." The instruments for destruction are in our hands *now*. The United Nations have the force to rule that global air *now*. In the light of these facts, the Marshal believes that a commercial battle for air traffic among the Allies would be suicidal. "No man of good will can support a world-aviation operated by profit-seeking individuals and founded on the dog-eat-dog theory of commerce. The air is not national. . . . No words can be minced about it. The air-world must be world-controlled."

"The flying machine," says Charles G. Bolte, "has revolutionized geography and abolished national frontiers and strategic barriers. . . . Unless the world air is world controlled, we had better start digging deeper shelters."[9] If Bishop and Bolte are right, and I think both soldiers know what they are talking about, the present row over boundaries in Europe sounds as antiquated as a muzzle-loading cannon.

8. *Winged Peace,* Viking, New York, 1944.
9. *The Nation,* November 18, 1944.

What good to Russia are the Baltic States, East Poland, Bessarabia, if a 1950 model V-3 can vaporize the Kremlin three and a half hours after it leaves Newfoundland? Of what earthly use is the Rhineland to France as a buffer state, or Thrace to Greece, or a corridor to Poland? All these bickerings about odd pieces of real estate are rapidly becoming antediluvian. It looks as if our only chance were to make sure that no group anywhere can use one cubic foot of the world's air, except on peaceful missions.

If this were done, then a V-2 might be put to useful work. J. B. S. Haldane suggests that if fired vertically, without a warhead, V-2 might rise 200 miles and take such photographs of the sun and stars as no eye has ever seen. "For the cost of a day at war, it should be practicable to send a series of rockets around the moon and photograph its far side."[10]

Winged Peace or Winged Death?

It is impossible to discuss foreign trade without reference to these two technological developments, one bright, one dark, which have been fighting for mastery since the industrial revolution began. Indeed, trade is a function of these forces.

If the bright side wins out, and atomic bricks fulfill their destiny, the continents, if not the nations, will be far more self-sufficient in essential raw materials than ever before. Trade will completely change its character. But if the several nations produce specialties of textiles, leather work, glassware, wines, dye stuffs, instruments of precision, silver work, scenery, which other people want, or want to see, there is no reason why the volume of international commerce should not be healthy.

10. *Time,* November 27, 1944.

If the dark side wins out, and winged death hovers over all of us, foreign commerce will be a small problem. The real problem will be how to get a thousand feet of earth between one's anatomy and the warhead of the approaching manless projectile, the sound of whose flight will never reach our ears.